250 Grammatik-Übungen
ENGLISCH

Für Anfänger und Fortgeschrittene.
Mit ausführlichen Lösungen.

von
Christina Cott

PONS GmbH
Stuttgart

PONS
250 Grammatik-Übungen
ENGLISCH

Für Anfänger und Fortgeschrittene. Mit ausführlichen Lösungen.

von
Christina Cott

1. Auflage 2017

Redaktion: Dr. Birgit Reinel
Logoentwurf: Erwin Poell, Heidelberg
Logoüberarbeitung: Sabine Redlin, Ludwigsburg
Einbandgestaltung: Anne Helbich, Stuttgart
Layout: Petra Michel, Gestaltung & Typografie, Essen
Satz: Digraf.pl - dtp services
Druck und Bindung: Multiprint GmbH

Printed in the EU.
ISBN: 978-3-12-562880-9

WILLKOMMEN

Mit den **250 Grammatik-Übungen ENGLISCH** können Sie in kleinen Portionen und wo immer Sie wollen Ihre Grammatikkenntnisse trainieren und festigen oder auffrischen. Dabei erfahren Sie auch viel Wissenswertes zu den Themen, die Sie üben möchten.

Von leicht bis schwer

Die Übungen sind nach Grammatikthemen sortiert, damit Sie gezielt nach Ihren persönlichen Bedürfnissen üben können. Zu jedem Thema stehen Ihnen Übungen in drei Schwierigkeitsstufen zur Verfügung:

★ = leicht

★★ = mittelschwer

★★★ = schwer

Erweitern Sie nebenbei Ihr Grammatikwissen

Zahlreiche Tipps weisen Sie auf wichtige Ausnahmen, Stolperfallen, typische Fehler und schwierige Regeln hin und helfen Ihnen bei der Lösung einer Übung.

! = Infos zu Ausnahmen und Stolperfallen

= weiterführende Erklärungen

= Hinweise zu Aussprache und Betonung

ABC = Angaben zum Wortschatz

So überprüfen Sie Ihren Lernfortschritt

Anhand der **Lösungen** ab Seite 148 können Sie Ihren Lernfortschritt überprüfen. Übungen, in denen Sie noch nicht ganz fehlerfrei waren, wiederholen Sie einfach nach einiger Zeit.

Setzen Sie vorne im **Inhaltsverzeichnis** einen Haken hinter alle Themen, die Sie erledigt haben. So können Sie auf einen Blick sehen, wie viel Sie schon trainiert haben.

Unbekannte Wörter? Kein Problem!

Alle Wörter und Wendungen aus den Übungen können Sie in der englisch-deutschen **Wortliste** ab Seite 166 nachschlagen.

Lernvideos

Zu diesen Grammatik-Übungen stehen Ihnen mehrere Lernvideos online zur Verfügung, in denen Ihnen ein Sprachlehrer wichtige grammatische Phänomene erklärt.

Gehen Sie auf **www.pons.de/250-grammatik-englisch** und lernen Sie weiter!

Viel Erfolg!
Ihre PONS-Redaktion

INHALT

GRAMMATISCHE FACHBEGRIFFE

Englisch	Latein/Deutsch
adjective	Adjektiv, Eigenschaftswort
adverb	Adverb, Umstandswort
auxiliary verb	Hilfsverb
comparative	Komparativ, 1. Steigerungsstufe
conditional	Konditional, Bedingungsform
conjunction	Konjunktion, Bindewort
definite article	bestimmter Artikel, bestimmtes Geschlechtswort
direct object	direktes Objekt
future tense	Futur, Zukunft
genitive	Genitiv, 2. Fall
gerund	Gerundium, gebeugter Infinitiv
imperative	Imperativ, Befehlsform
indefinite article	unbestimmter Artikel, unbestimmtes Geschlechtswort
indirect object	indirektes Objekt
infinitive	Infinitiv, Grundform des Verbs
modal verb	modales Hilfsverb
noun	Nomen, Hauptwort, Substantiv
participle	Partizip, Mittelwort
past tense	Präteritum, Vergangenheit
plural	Plural, Mehrzahl
predicate	Prädikat, Satzaussage
preposition	Präposition, Verhältniswort
present tense	Präsens, Gegenwart
present perfect	Perfekt, vollendete Gegenwart
progressive form	Verlaufsform
pronoun	Pronomen, Fürwort
question tag	Bestätigungsfrage
relative clause	Relativsatz
reported/indirect speech	indirekte Rede
singular	Einzahl
subject	Subjekt, Satzgegenstand
superlative	Superlativ, 2. Steigerungsstufe, Höchststufe
tense	Tempus, Zeitform
verb	Verb, Tätigkeitswort, Tunwort
word order	Wortstellung

Geschlecht, Berufe und Anrede

1 ★

He, **she** oder **it**? Welches **Geschlecht** haben die folgenden Substantive? Achtung: Einige können sowohl weiblich (w) als auch männlich (m) sein.

a)	mum	(w/~~m/s~~)	**g)**	taxi driver	(w/m/s)
b)	uncle	(w/m/s)	**h)**	rat	(w/m/s)
c)	teacher	(w/m/s)	**i)**	guest	(w/m/s)
d)	waiter	(w/m/s)	**j)**	computer	(w/m/s)
e)	fantasy	(w/m/s)	**k)**	our dog Rex	(w/m/s)
f)	friend	(w/m/s)	**l)**	secretary	(w/m/s)

2 ★★

Wie lauten die weiblichen Formen der folgenden **Berufsbezeichnungen**?

a)	pilot	*pilot*	**g)**	businessman	______
b)	steward	______	**h)**	author	______
c)	waiter	______	**i)**	chemist	______
d)	shop assistant	______	**j)**	househusband	______
e)	fireman	______	**k)**	dentist	______
f)	actor	______	**l)**	postman	______

ABC

Mit den Zusätzen **male/female** oder **man/woman** kann man verdeutlichen, welches Geschlecht ein Substantiv hat, z. B. a **male manager**, a **woman doctor**.

Beachten Sie, dass im Englischen vor Berufsbezeichnungen immer der unbestimmte Artikel steht, z. B.:

She's **a pilot**. *Sie ist Pilotin (von Beruf).*

3 Übersetzen Sie und beachten Sie dabei die Fälle (Nominativ, Akkusativ, Dativ).

★

a) *Der Junge ist sechzehn.*

____

b) *Der Lehrer spricht mit dem Jungen.*

____

c) *Die Mutter ruft den Jungen.*

____

4 Vervollständigen Sie den Text mit den richtigen **Groß- und Kleinbuchstaben**.

★★

Some C/c_c_ountries **(a)** are very popular for W/w__inter H/h__olidays **(b)**. For E/e__xample **(c)**, many G/g__ermans **(d)** travel to A/a__ustria **(e)** at C/c__hristmas **(f)** and on N/n__ew Y/y__ear's D/d__ay **(g)**. But also P/p__eople **(h)** from the N/n__etherlands **(i)** make the long J/j__ourney **(j)** to go S/s__kiing **(k)** there. However, the F/f__rench **(l)** and the I/i__talians **(m)** prefer to stay at H/h__ome **(n)** to ski.

In S/s__pring **(o)**, there is usually also a R/r__un **(p)** on the H/h__otels **(q)** in the A/a__lps **(r)** and especially over E/e__aster **(s)** the A/a__ustrian M/m__ountains **(t)** are overcrowded. The S/s__ame **(u)** is true for S/s__aturdays and S/s__undays **(v)** in F/f__ebruary, M/m__arch and A/a__pril **(w)**. However, the A/a__rea **(x)** is also popular in the S/s__ummer M/m__onths **(y)**. Many T/t__ravellers **(z)** enjoy C/c__ity **(ab)** T/t__rips **(ac)** to V/v__ienna **(ad)** or L/l__ake C/c__onstance **(ae)** and C/c__ruises **(af)** on the D/d__anube **(ag)**.

ABC

In den Überschriften von amerikanischen Texten werden Substantive, Verben, Adjektive und Adverbien meist groß geschrieben. Wer sich nicht sicher ist, schreibt am besten die ganze Überschrift in Großbuchstaben.

5 ★★★

Wie lautet die korrekte englische **Anrede** (bzw. der korrekte Titel)?

a) ______________________________ *(Frau Prof. Schmidt)* is giving a series of lectures at the University of London this term.

b) Allow me to introduce ______________________________ *(Frau Dr. und Herr Dr. Moose)* from Yorkshire.

c) ______________________________ *(Herr und Frau Vogel)* go on holiday to Cornwall every year.

d) And now – ______________________________ *(der Präsident der Vereinigten Staaten von Amerika)*!

Singular und Plural

6 ★

Wie bildet man die **Pluralformen** der folgenden Wörter?

a) dress *dresses*

b) city ____________

c) dish ____________

d) sister-in-law ____________

e) grandchild ____________

f) firewoman ____________

g) quiz ____________

h) tomato ____________

i) fish ____________

j) church ____________

7 ★★

Wie lauten diese Begriffe im Englischen?

a) *zwei Schwägerinnen* ____________

b) *wenige Zähne* ____________

c) *zwei Füße* ____________

d) *ein paar Mäuse und Gänse* ____________

8 ★★★

Achtung Glatteis: Folgt auf die englischen Gruppenbezeichnungen ein Verb im **Singular** oder **Plural**? Kreisen Sie die jeweils richtige Form ein.

Bühl football team **has / have (a)** worked together well. A lot of people **is / are (b)** curious because of this surprise success. Their coach says that the team **is / are (c)** like a large family. "A true family **works / work (d)** together when they need each other. That's it." A class from the local school **has / have (e)** watched the game, and they all want to join some team or other now.

9 ★★★

Übersetzen Sie die folgenden Werbeslogans ins Englische.

a) **Die Polizei sucht Sie!**

____

b) **Kaufen Sie eine Jeans und erhalten Sie eine kostenlos dazu!**

____

c) **Diese Schere schneidet einfach alles!**

____

d) **Die Nachrichten? ... kommen auf Kanal FastFox!**

____

ABC

Manchmal ist im Englischen keine Pluralform möglich, z. B. **hair** - *Haar(e)*, **fruit** - *Früchte*. Oder die Pluralform hat eine andere Bedeutung, z. B. **fruits** - *Obstsorten*.

10 ★

Welche jeweils zwei Sätze mit **nicht zählbaren Substantiven** sind falsch?

a) ☐ A We need milk. ☐ B We need a milk.

☐ C We need some milks. ☐ D We need a bottle of milk.

b) ☐ A The informations in this leaflet aren't very helpful.

☐ B The information in this leaflet isn't very helpful.

☐ C Some pieces of information in this leaflet aren't very helpful.

☐ D An information in this leaflet isn't very helpful.

11 ★★

Welche Mengenangaben können mit den **nicht zählbaren Substantiven** auf den Fotos verwendet werden? Manchmal gibt es mehrere Möglichkeiten.

a bar of • a bottle of • a cup of • a glass of • a jar of • a loaf of • a packet of • a piece of • a pot of • a slice of

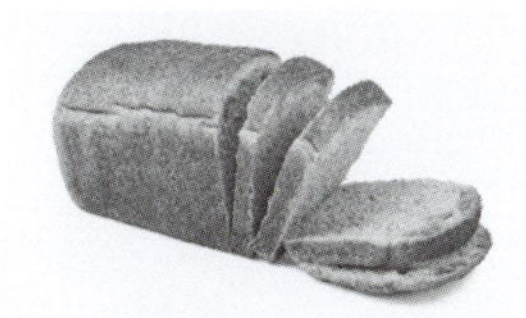

a) bread: *a slice of,* *a loaf of*

b) fruit: ____________ ____________

c) music: ____________ ____________

d) tea: ____________ ____________

e) chocolate: ____________ ____________

f) milk: ____________ ____________

g) cake: ____________ ____________

h) jam: ____________ ____________

i) luggage: ____________ ____________

12 ★★

Können Sie die folgenden Sätze mit der passenden **unbestimmten Mengenangabe** ergänzen? Manchmal gibt es mehrere richtige Lösungen.

a lot of ▪ any ▪ enough ▪ little ▪ much ▪ no ▪ not much ▪ some

a) I can't give you ______________________ advice.

b) We don't have ______________________ time to visit you.

c) We have ______________________ old furniture.

d) Do you have ______________________ money?

e) We had ______________________ snow last week.

f) She still has ______________________ news about her cat.

g) There's ______________________ water left in the tank.

13 ★★★

Tragen Sie die jeweils passenden **unbestimmten Mengenangaben** an den angegebenen Stellen im Kreuzworträtsel ein.

a) We have ... new furniture.

b) How ... rooms does your new flat have?

c) Do you have ... room?

d) How ... space is in the attic?

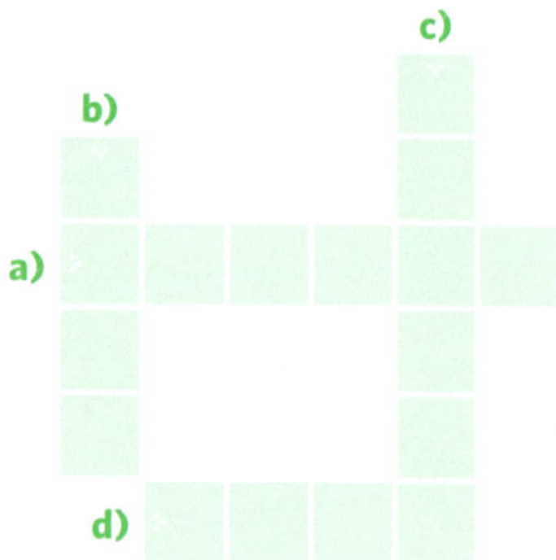

Genitiv

14 ★ Welche der drei Ausdrücke sind jeweils korrekt? Kreuzen Sie sie an.

a) ☐ A Marina's book
☐ B Marinas book
☐ C Marinas' book

b) ☐ A my parent's neighbours
☐ B my parents' neighbour
☐ C my parents neighbours

c) ☐ A the dogs hut
☐ B the dog's hut
☐ C the dogs' huts

d) ☐ A the house of the Mitchells
☐ B the house of the Mitchells'
☐ C the Mitchells' house

Geht es um Städte, Nationen, Institutionen oder allgemein menschliche Gemeinschaften, kann statt des ***of*-Genitivs** auch der ***s*-Genitiv** verwendet werden, z. B. Berlin**'s** opera houses; Austria**'s** mountains; the school**'s** rules.

15 ★ Ordnen Sie die passenden Teile von **Genitiv-Ausdrücken** einander zu.

a) at the
b) Mr Schmidt's
c) let's meet at
d) yesterday's
e) little Marcus'
f) the neighbours'
g) the children's
h) the name

___ A Marion's
___ B toy car
___ C newspaper
___ D tricycles
___ E of the street
___ F lawn mower
___ G gardens
a) H baker's

16 ★★

Setzen Sie s, 's, nur ' oder gar nichts ein.

a) How did the chef___ dish___ taste?

b) Jess___ bag must be in one of the kid___ room___.

c) Did you take back the Jones___ tennis racket___?

d) Have you been to the doctor___ to check on that problem of your___?

e) The pilot___ union demands higher wage___ from the airline___ bosses___.

17 ★★★

Daniel möchte einem Freund, der in Neuseeland studiert, eine E-Mail schreiben. Wie lauten die Ausdrücke in Klammern richtig auf Englisch?

From: ______ To: ______

Hello Steve,

I'm writing to tell you that ______________________________ **(a)** *(ein Freund meines Bruders)* knows your professor. Mike says ______________________________ **(b)** *(die Seminarthemen von Professor Marcus)* are ______________________________ **(c)** *(einige der schwersten)*. And what's more, he did ______________________________ **(d)** *(einen der Kurse deines Professors)* and says it's almost impossible to pass ______________________________ **(e)** *(eine seiner Prüfungen)*.

By the way, do you know the Robertsons? Mike stayed with them and says they have become ______________________________ **(f)** *(gute Freunde von ihm)*. If you like, you could visit them and tell them you are ______________________________ **(g)** *(ein Freund eines Freundes von Mike)*. He says they will be happy to help you with ______________________________ **(h)** *(dieser Seminararbeit von dir)*.

Best wishes,
Daniel

18 ★

Suchen Sie mögliche deutsche Übersetzungen für den bestimmten Artikel **the** im Wortgitter (waagerecht oder senkrecht) und markieren Sie sie.

w	a	s	e	l	f	i	n	d	a
i	d	e	r	m	e	i	n	a	n
e	u	c	e	w	r	d	e	s	v
s	o	d	i	e	s	e	s	w	o
d	e	i	n	r	i	s	u	i	n
e	u	e	e	w	e	s	n	e	v
m	l	f	n	d	e	n	s	e	o

19 ★

Achtung Glatteis: Der **bestimmte Artikel** hat zwei Aussprachevarianten, je nach Anfangslaut des darauf folgenden Substantivs. Ordnen Sie zu.

the abbey • the bank • the building • the entrance • the hospital • the hour • the house • the institution • the minute • the object • the office • the surgery • the underground • the university

the [ðə]	the [ði:] / [ði]

Bei besonderer Betonung wird der bestimmte Artikel ebenfalls **[ði:]** gesprochen, z. B.: 'Marketplace' is **the [ði:]** website for second-hand articles.

20 ★

Markieren Sie den richtigen unbestimmten Artikel: **a** oder **an**.

a) a/an noun
b) a/an uncountable noun
c) a/an book
d) a/an exciting book
e) a/an scene
f) a/an horrible scene

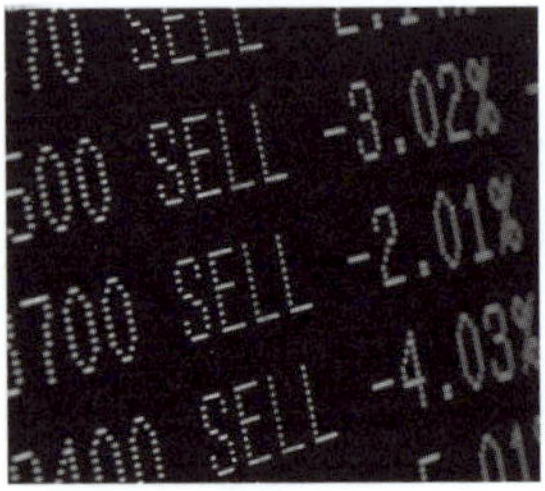

g) a/an interview
h) a/an boring interview
i) a/an order
j) a/an accurate order
k) a/an honour
l) a/an unexpected honour

Die Aussprache des betonten unbestimmten Artikels **a/an** lautet: **[eɪ]** / **[æn]**.

21 ★★

Setzen Sie den unbestimmten Artikel **a/an** oder nichts ein.

My friend Chiara is ____ **(a)** Italian. She works for Air Italia as ____ **(b)** stewardess. Her husband Björn is ____ **(c)** captain with Air Italia. He is from Northern Germany and is ____ **(d)** Protestant. Chiara's mother had been a bit anxious about their marriage at first as she is ____ **(e)** mayor of a small town where all the people are ____ **(f)** Roman Catholics. But then she said that as she could never become ____ **(g)** pope anyway, the gossip didn't really matter.

!

Anders als im Deutschen wird der unbestimmte Artikel auch benötigt bei Ausdrücken wie z. B. to have **a headache** – *Kopfschmerzen haben*; to be in **a hurry** – *in Eile sein*.

22 ★★

Wie wird der **bestimmte Artikel in Verbindung mit Namen** verwendet? Kreuzen Sie die richtigen Sätze an.

a) ☐ A Loch Ness is the most famous Scottish lake.
☐ B The Loch Ness is the most famous Scottish lake.

b) ☐ A Many people visit Isle of Wight to go sailing.
☐ B Many people visit the Isle of Wight to go sailing.

c) ☐ A Buckingham Palace is London's most popular sight.
☐ B The Buckingham Palace is London's most popular sight.

d) ☐ A We sailed across North Sea and English Channel right into Thames.
☐ B We sailed across the North Sea and the English Channel right into the Thames.

e) ☐ A The poor Grandma always loses her glasses.
☐ B Poor Grandma always loses her glasses.

f) ☐ A Jane, Peter and the Sheridans came to dinner last night.
☐ B The Jane, the Peter and the Sheridans came to dinner last night.

g) ☐ A The Mont Blanc in the France is the highest mountain in the Alps.
☐ B Mont Blanc in France is the highest mountain in the Alps.

h) ☐ A The Hyde Park in England and the Central Park in United States both are very popular.
☐ B Hyde Park in England and Central Park in the United States both are very popular.

23

★★★

Verbinden Sie die Satzteile sinnvoll miteinander.

a) Joe often stays up all	___ A dark.
b) He doesn't mind staying up in	___ B a day at a time.
c) Joe likes	___ C morning.
d) He seems to work better after	___ D the night.
e) Often he is still working by	___ E the dark.
f) He usually goes to bed in	___ F night.
g) Joe just goes on vacation for	___ G a dark night.
h) But sometimes he stays for	___ H the morning.

24

★★★

Bringen Sie die Wörter in die richtige Reihenfolge.

a) in | Let's | hour | an | garden | for | half | sit | the

___

b) the | What | nice | all | afternoon | full | with | flowers | in | bloom | a

___

c) so warm | It's | summer | that | quite | a | is | the | surprise

___

d) last year | froze | It was | the | such | that | a cold winter | lake

___

e) wasps | last summer | Half | is flying around | the | compared to | number of

___

___

!

Der Artikel wird bei **too** + **adjective** nachgestellt, z. B.:

This is too difficult **a** path for a small child. – *... ein zu schwieriger Wanderweg ...*

25 ★★★

Artikel oder kein Artikel? Übersetzen Sie.

a) *Wir trinken oft Wein beim Abendessen. Ich mag Wein aus Südafrika.*

______

b) *Das Leben kann aufregend sein. Ich lese gerade ein Buch über Winston Churchills Leben.*

______

c) *Tom wird im Herbst aufs College gehen. Er wird mit dem Bus hinfahren.*

______

d) *Ich muss mein Smartphone im Zug vergessen haben.*

______

e) *Das Essen im Hotel war gut, aber ich bevorzuge italienisches Essen.*

______

f) *Mia liest gerne Bücher. Ihr Mann liest nur Zeitung.*

______

g) *Wir gehen gewöhnlich am Wochenende zum Abendessen aus.*

______

!

Wird **most** im Sinne von „die Mehrzahl/die meisten" verwendet, steht es ohne Artikel (nicht wie im Deutschen „die meisten"), z. B.:

Most mobile phones include a camera these days. – *Die meisten Mobiltelefone ...*

26 Welcher Satz ist jeweils korrekt? Kreuzen Sie an.

★

a) ☐ A John never buys apples.
☐ B John never buys some apples.
☐ C John never buys any apples.

b) ☐ A I made any salad for lunch.
☐ B I made some salad for lunch.
☐ C I made salad for lunch.

c) ☐ A I can't see some snow.
☐ D I can't see snow.
☐ C I can't see any snow.

d) ☐ A Mary seldom has money.
☐ B Mary seldom has some money.
☐ C Mary seldom has any money.

!

Anders als im Deutschen kann bei einer unbestimmten Menge oder Anzahl die Mengenangabe im Englischen nicht weggelassen werden, z. B.:

Can you lend me **some money**, please? *Kannst du mir (etwas) Geld leihen?*

27 Was ist hier richtig: **some** oder **any**?

★

a) We don't want **some / any** soup.
b) I'd really like **some / any** beer with my meal.
c) Waiter, could I have **some / any** salt, please?
d) Would you like **some / any** of this wine? It's really good!
e) Do you have **some / any** Belgian beer? I can't find it on the menu.
f) Could you bring us **some / any** more bread, please?
g) Do you have **some / any** beef sausages, or only these pork sausages?

!

Nach Wörtern, die eine Verneinung ausdrücken, wie z. B. **rarely/seldom**, **scarcely/hardly**, **not** und **never**, folgt **any** (nicht **some**!):

There are **rarely any** koala bears in our garden.
Es sind selten (irgendwelche) Koalabären in unserem Garten.

28 ★

Die Satzteile sind durcheinandergeraten. Ordnen Sie sie zu.

a) Do you spend much	___ A chocolate left.
b) Do you read many	___ B photos for a good album.
c) I have eaten	___ C guests.
d) We have very little	___ D chocolates left.
e) There are too few	___ E trifle.
f) But Martin takes a lot of	___ F eggs, please?
g) The hotel here hasn't many	___ G novels at university?
h) There must be plenty of	___ H news about the events in Iran.
i) No, there's only a little	___ I photos.
j) Mary, could I borrow a few	___ J money on books?

!

(not) **much**	– *(nicht) viel*
(a) little	– *(ein) wenig* + nicht zählbare Substantive
(not) **many**	– *(nicht) viele*
few	– *wenige*
a few	– *ein paar* + Substantive im Plural

29 ★★

Wandeln Sie die folgenden Sätze in **verneinte Sätze** um.

a) Grandma has seen a man somewhere outside.

____

b) Surely Jane knows something else about the case.

____

c) The police will ask some questions in the neighbourhood.

____

d) The neighbours might have seen somebody.

____

e) But the man will already be somewhere else.

____

ABC

Nach Zusammensetzungen mit **some** bzw. **any** kann ein Adjektiv oder **else** stehen:

Does he know **anything interesting** about the case? *... irgendetwas Interessantes ...?*
Let's ask **somebody else**. *... jemand anderes ...*

30 ★★

Vervollständigen Sie den Dialog mit den Wörtern in der Box.

any • anybody • anything • anywhere • nobody • none • nothing • nowhere • some • somebody • something • somewhere

Lucy: Hey, Matt. What about our holiday? Have Gina and you had ____________ **(a)** idea yet where we should go?

Matt: You know, I would go almost ____________ **(b)**. Unfortunately, Gina liked ____________ **(c)** of the proposals I made. She thinks it should be

_______________ **(d)** special, where _______________ **(e)** else she knows has been to.

Jim: Wow! Did she say _______________ **(f)** more detailed?

Matt: No, she wanted to talk to _______________ **(g)** today to get _______________ **(h)** more information first.

Gina: Matt, Lucy, Jim, where are you? I've got to tell you _______________ **(i)**! The travel agent told me that hardly _______________ **(j)** ever travels to Pitcairn. She says it's like _______________ **(k)** else on the planet!

Matt: Well, it seems there's _______________ **(l)** we can do but book now ...

31 ★★★

Bilden Sie Sätze aus den Bruchstücken.

a) gardens | to | two | belong | hobby gardeners | most | both | passionate

____

b) beautiful | gardens | the | but | grumblers | are | gardeners | their | are | two

____

c) and | now they | of | both | retired | their hobby | them | are | focus on

____

d) cares to | neither | smile at | them | even | anybody, | of | children | not

____

e) friendly | haven't | of | seen | we | them | for years | being | either

____

!

Anders als im Deutschen ist **both** immer betont und steht nie nach einem bestimmten Artikel. Für das unbetonte „die beiden/die zwei“ verwendet man **the two**, z. B.:

Both dogs stay inside at night, but	*Beide Hunde ...*
the two cats often go for a walk.	*... die beiden ...*

32

★★

Was ist hier richtig: **all** oder **all the**?

a) **All / All the** vegetables should be eaten freshly.

b) Otherwise **all / all the** vitamins in them will be lost.

c) Our children love **all / all the** animals on our farm.

d) Dad has worked **all / all the** week on that tree house.

e) **All / All the** children love tree houses.

f) Tim spent **all / all the** his money on a motorbike.

g) **All / All the** money is circulating constantly.

!

every + Substantiv	*jede(r/s) allgemein oder in beschränkter Anzahl*
each (meist mit *of*-Genitiv oder Substantiv)	*jede(r/s) einzelne aus einer Gruppe*
any + Substantiv; **anybody**	*jede(r/s) beliebige*

33

★★★

Übersetzen Sie die folgenden Sätze ins Englische.

a) *Wir kauften jedem der Kinder ein Eis.*

____

b) *Jedes Kindergartenkind hat den Besuch im Märchenpark geliebt.*

____

c) *Jeder mag Amy, die freundliche Kindergärtnerin.*

____

d) *Mike geht im Sommer jedes Wochenende surfen.*

____

e) *Jedes der Hotelzimmer hat ein separates Badezimmer.*

____

f) *Du kannst uns jederzeit besuchen, wenn du in der Stadt bist.*

____

g) *Du kannst jeden Zug oder Bus nach Stuttgart nehmen.*

____

h) *Am Hauptbahnhof kannst du jeden nach dem Weg zur U-Bahn fragen.*

____

34 ★★★

Lösen Sie das Kreuzworträtsel. Die Buchstaben in den markierten Feldern ergeben ein weiteres Mengenwort.

a) Unbestimmtes Mengenwort in verneinten Aussagesätzen.

b) Welches Mengenwort steht statt **many** mit unzählbaren Substantiven?

c) Welches Mengenwort kann die Kombination **not ... anything** ersetzen?

d) Welches Mengenwort steht statt **little** mit Substantiven im Plural?

e) Mengenwort zur unbestimmten Angabe eines Ortes in bejahten Sätzen.

f) Welches Mengenwort ersetzt die Kombination **not ... either**?

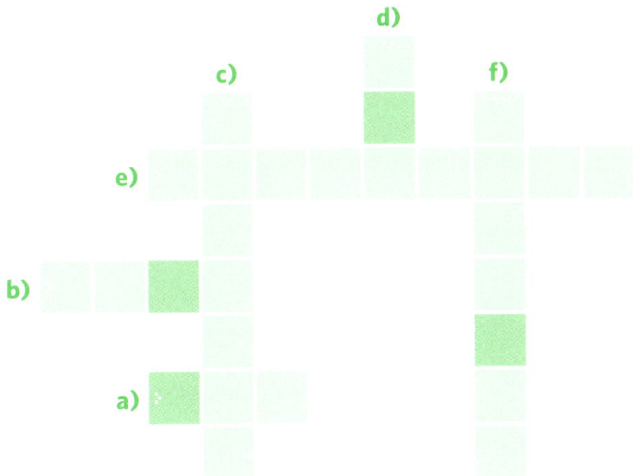

Lösungswort: ______________________________

Personalpronomen

35 ★

Wer ist gemeint? Ordnen Sie die Bilder den Sätzen zu und schreiben Sie das passende **Personalpronomen** in die Lücke.

_F_ **a)** _We_ are married.

___ **b)** _____ is a teacher.

___ **c)** Tom and _____ are 35 years old.

___ **d)** Thank _____ for coming. Cheers!

___ **e)** _____ is a doctor.

___ **f)** _____ are talking.

36 ★

Schreiben Sie das richtige **Objektpronomen** in die Lücke.

her • it • her • me • it • her • us • it • you

a) Jane and I had a cup of coffee today and talked. I think she likes _____.

b) Have you seen the new sculpture on the campus? I don't like _____.

c) Tom phones Kate every day. He misses _____ terribly.

d) We would like to see you again. Please visit _____!

e) I would like to have an animal. But I haven't got enough room for ______.

f) This is our cat Josie. If she hides, it's not easy to find ______.

g) Have you put the car into the garage? – Yes, and I've locked ______.

h) Did you hear about the Titanic? They've located ______ on the seabed.

Bei einer besonderen Beziehung verwendet man auch männliche oder weibliche Pronomen für Tiere und weibliche Pronomen für Schiffe, Autos u.ä.

Our dog Rocky is a Labrador. **He** loves to fetch things from the water.
This is the Gorch Fock. **She**'s the second ship of that name.

37 ★★

Die Sätze sind durcheinandergeraten. Ordnen Sie sie und achten Sie dabei auf die **Stellung der Objekte** und **Objektpronomen**.

a) bank statement | me | has sent | the bank | my

____

b) customers | gives | the financial adviser | good advice | her

____

c) your | tell | you | account number | can | me | ?

____

d) the cash machine | me | the bank cashier | was showing

____

e) to | the bill | I | my wife | gave

____

f) I | Ben claims | he | am | faster than | him | me | but | as fast as | is

____

38 ★★★

Formulieren Sie die Sätze um und verwenden Sie dabei ein passendes **allgemeines Personalpronomen**.

one ▪ people ▪ they ▪ you

a) It is necessary to be sure of the facts before publishing them.

b) Nobody will ever know.

c) Smoking is not allowed in this lounge.

d) The persons responsible should meet and find a solution.

ABC

Allgemeine Personalpronomen können jede beliebige Person bezeichnen und entsprechen dem Deutschen „man".

one (formaler Sprachgebrauch) **you** (Umgangssprache)	schließen den Sprecher mit ein
they **people**	beziehen sich auf (mehrere) andere, unbekannte Personen oder eine bestimmte Gruppe

Possessivpronomen und -begleiter

39 ★

Finden Sie die **Possessivbegleiter und -pronomen** in der Wortschlange.

rthey'rehisitsmeyouminewhoseoursit'syoursthemthattheirshimhersourhethemys

40 ★★

Welcher der beiden Sätze ist jeweils richtig? Kreuzen Sie an.

a) ☐ A They are friends of mine.
☐ B They are friends of mines.

b) ☐ A It's warm, so you won't need your coat.
☐ B It's warm, so you won't need a coat.

c) ☐ A Raise the hands if you know answer.
☐ B Raise your hands if you know the answer.

d) ☐ A Cats follow own rules.
☐ B Cats follow their own rules.

e) ☐ A I own a convertible. It's top is a nice burgundy red.
☐ B I own a convertible. Its top is a nice burgundy red.

f) ☐ A Mrs Myers, have you lost your handbag?
☐ B Mrs Myers, have you lost her handbag?

41 ★★★

Übersetzen Sie die folgenden Sätze ins Englische.

a) *Vor kurzem hatte Tom noch kein eigenes Auto. Jetzt hat er ein eigenes.*

____

b) *Wessen Notizen sind das? Ihre oder die Ihres Mitstudenten?*

____

!

Mit **own** betont man die Zugehörigkeit zu etwas/jemandem. **Own** steht immer mit einem Possessivbegleiter. Es gibt dabei zwei Möglichkeiten der Satzstellung:

I've got **my own laptop** now. I've got **a laptop of my own** now.

Reflexivpronomen

42 ★

Ordnen Sie den vorgegebenen Personen, Gegenständen und Begriffen das passende **Reflexivpronomen** zu und übersetzen Sie es ins Deutsche.

herself • himself • itself • ourselves • themselves • yourself • yourselves

	English	German
a) Tom	*himself*	*(er) sich selbst*
b) a mouse		
c) Mr and Mrs Smith		
d) Tom's dog Mikey		
e) Tom and Mikey		
f) Ms Hill, Tom's teacher		
g) two desks		
h) you		
i) Tom, Mikey and me		
j) Tom and you		
k) an idea		

43 ★★

Verbinden Sie die jeweils passenden Satzteile.

a) Let Katie try it	___ A one another.
b) One should keep secrets to	___ B themselves.
c) Josie! Behave	___ C myself.
d) We built this house all by	___ D yourselves!

e)	Help me! Robert has just cut	___ **E**	himself?
f)	The men will enjoy	___ **F**	herself.
g)	Don't worry, the barbecue can take care of	___ **G**	oneself.
h)	Steve, Matt, I believe you know	___ **H**	himself.
i)	Mia and Lisa, take care of	___ **I**	ourselves.
j)	Neighbours usually help	___ **J**	each other?
k)	Are you sure it doesn't work? I repaired it	___ **K**	itself.
l)	Did you manage to speak to the mayor	___ **L**	yourself.

44 ★★★

Jemand hat bei der Übersetzung eines Textes ins Englische alle reflexiven Verben ausgelassen. Können Sie die Verben korrekt einsetzen?

We planned *to build* ________ **(a)** *(uns … bauen;* **infinitive***)* a tree house for *ourselves* ________ **(b)**. When Dad heard about it, he ________ **(c)** *(sich darauf freuen;* **past progressive***)* helping us. He ________ **(d)** *(sich wundern;* **past simple***)* that we ________ **(e)** *(uns ansehen;* **past simple***)* and had to grin. We ________ **(f)** *(uns vorstellen;* **past simple***)* how Dad would help us with his two left hands. Of course we ________ **(g)** *(uns freuen;* **past simple***)* about his offer. Dad and us, we ________ **(h)** *(uns lieben;* **present simple***)*! But it is simply better if Dad ________ **(i)** *(sich fernhalten;* **present simple***)* from any tools.

ABC

Die Abkürzung DIY findet man z. B. auf Produktpaketen zum Selbermachen.

DIY = Do it **yourself**!	*Mach/Machen Sie es selbst!*
Behave **yourself**!	*Benimm dich!/Benehmen Sie sich!*
Enjoy **yourself**!	*Viel Spaß!*
Help **yourself**!	*Bedien dich!/Bedienen Sie sich!*

Demonstrativpronomen und -begleiter

45 ★

Welches **Demonstrativpronomen** bzw. welcher **Demonstrativbegleiter** ist jeweils richtig? Einige können mehrfach verwendet werden.

that ▪ these ▪ this ▪ those

a) I want to go into ________ shops on the other side of the street.

b) ________ shirt is too small. Don't I look terrible in it?

c) I'd like to exchange ________ trousers for the ones over there.

d) ________ department store in Blue Street is too hot. Let's not go there.

e) Long skirts are very fashionable ________ autumn.

f) ________ is my bag. I believe ________ bag over there must be yours.

g) Airports are such crowded places ________ days.

this, these für (räumlich/zeitlich/in der Vorstellung) nahe Personen/Dinge
that, those für (räumlich/zeitlich/in der Vorstellung) entferntere Personen/Dinge

46 ★★

Sie haben Freunde aus England zu Besuch und sind gemeinsam beim Einkaufen. Ergänzen Sie die Sätze anhand der Bilder mit den richtigen **Begleitern + Substantiv/Stützwort** oder nur **Pronomen**.

a) *This cheese* looks rather dry.

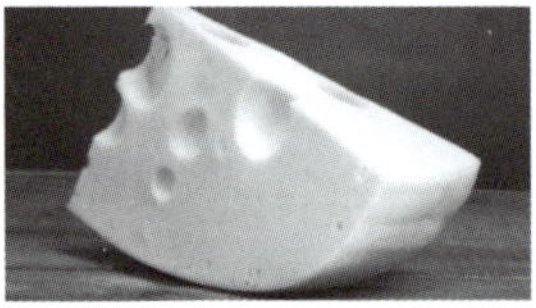

b) ________ looks better.

c) Hey, what about ________ over there?

d) We need some wine, too. What about ________?

e) I'd go for ________. It looks more French.

f) Look, ________ ________ will fit the wine fantastically.

g) Hm, ________ looks mouth-watering.

h) I'd prefer ________ as a main course.

i) I'd rather have ________ over there for dinner.

47 ★★★

Übersetzen Sie die folgenden Sätze. Achtung: Hier werden verschiedene **Pronomen** und **Begleiter** benötigt.

a) *Meine Eltern haben sich entschieden, diesen neuen Sport auszuprobieren.*

____

b) *Diese gelben Blumen habe ich selbst gepflanzt. Die da drüben nicht.*

____

c) *Welche von diesen Blusen soll ich mir kaufen? Die hier oder die da?*

____

d) *Das da drüben ist unser Wohnzimmer. Fühl dich wie zu Hause.*

____

ABC

In der Umgangssprache ist die Unterscheidung zwischen **this** und **that** nicht so wichtig, es sei denn, es geht um eine Gegenüberstellung.

48 ★

Sehen Sie sich die Bilder an und notieren Sie jeweils die englische **Präposition**, die die gezeigte Situation am besten beschreibt.

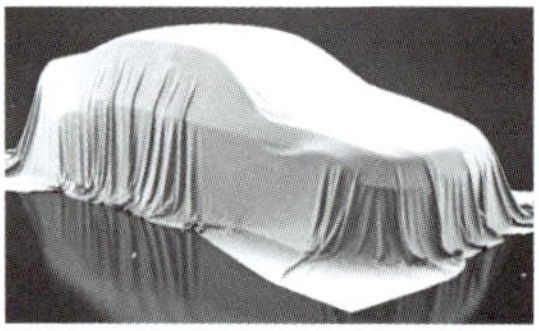

a) *under(neath)*

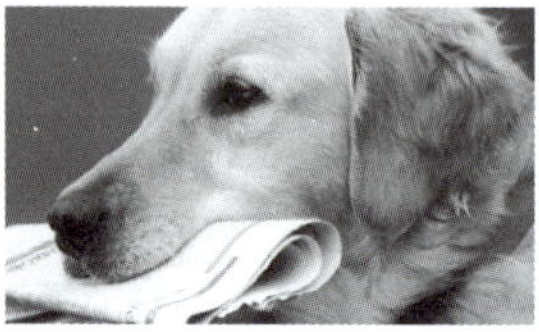

b) ______

c) ______

d) ______

e) ______

f) ______

g) ______

h) ______

i) ______

j) ______

k) ______

l) ______

!

Einige Ausdrücke mit Präpositionen darf man nicht einfach wörtlich übersetzen, sondern man muss sie sich merken, z. B.:

on the wall	*an der Wand*	**at the table**	*am/zu Tisch*
in the picture	*auf dem Bild*	**in the street/on the road**	*auf der Straße*

49 ★

Wählen Sie die jeweils passende **räumliche Präposition** aus und setzen Sie sie ein.

above • between • by • in • in front of • into • on • outside • round • to • under

The muesli's _on_ **(a)** the shelf ________ **(b)** the kitchen sideboard.

The apples are ________ **(c)** the fly screen ________ **(d)** the sideboard.

The bread bin is ________ **(e)** the food processor and the microwave.

If you're looking for the butter, the jam jar is ________ **(f)** it.

I placed the rubbish ________ **(g)** the door. I'll throw it ________ **(h)** the dustbin when I go ________ **(i)** the house. But it's raining.

To get ________ **(j)** the dustbin, you have to walk ________ **(k)** the house.

50 ★★

In diesem Wortgitter sind 20 **Präpositionen** versteckt. Können Sie sie alle finden? Achtung: Die Wörter können senkrecht, waagerecht und rückwärts stehen!

o	t	n	i	b	e	h	i	n	d
n	o	n	t	o	l	h	o	f	f
e	d	i	s	e	b	t	u	o	r
o	o	e	t	i	s	o	p	p	o
u	n	t	i	l	u	w	o	a	m
t	s	n	i	a	g	a	s	s	o
s	f	a	f	t	e	r	a	t	r
i	o	r	o	u	n	d	n	b	y
d	r	g	i	s	o	s	t	e	t
e	c	n	i	s	g	n	o	m	a

51 ★★

Vervollständigen Sie die Sätze, indem Sie die korrekte Kombination aus **Präposition mit Zeitangabe** auswählen.

a) Mark always reads the paper ...

- ☐ A at the morning.
- ☐ B at noon.
- ☐ C in the night.

b) My aunt will visit us ...

- ☐ A on Christmas.
- ☐ B on Christmas Day.
- ☐ C in the morning of December 25th.

c) We'll go skiing again ...

- ☐ A in next year.
- ☐ B 2016.
- ☐ C in the winter.

d) Helen's bus leaves ...

- ☐ A at 7 o'clock.
- ☐ B on 7 o'clock.
- ☐ C by 7 o'clock.

!

Stehen **next** oder **last** vor einem Zeitbegriff (z. B. Tag, Monat, Jahreszeit), wird keine Präposition benötigt:

He visited us **last June**. *Er besuchte uns (im) letzten Juni.*

52 ★★

Ergänzen Sie die Lücken mit den passenden **Präpositionen**.

Until **(a)** last year, Kate lived ________ **(b)** her parents. She had always wanted to live and study ________ **(c)** London. When she first came there, she stayed ________ **(d)** her cousin's. Of course this worked only ________ **(e)** a short time. Now she's living ________ **(f)** her boyfriend. They have been sharing a flat ________ **(g)** February. Luckily, the tube station is just ________ **(h)** the corner and the line stops ________ **(i)** the campus. ________ **(j)** that Kate was living ________ **(k)** a rented room. But there was always a lot of noise ________ **(l)** 6 p.m. and 10 p.m., so she couldn't concentrate on her studies.

53 ★★

Die Sätze sind durcheinandergeraten. Ordnen Sie die Wörter und achten Sie auf die richtige Stellung der **Präpositionen** im Satz.

a) at | let's meet | in front of | on | the zoo | by | 9 a.m. | Saturday | the pavilion

____

____

b) go | through | I'd like | too hot | by 10.30 | it's | the greenhouses | to | before

____

____

c) the hill | we can | walk | round | the sea lions' pool | on | past | and | go

____

d) before | we can | into | at | the elephants | going | look | the new ape house

____

____

e) it has been | in | open | April | for | a few weeks | since | its completion

____

f) 6 p.m. | the opening hours | from | have been | since | 9 a.m. | to | June

____

ABC

Sprichwörter und Redewendungen aus der Tierwelt:

Birds of a feather flock together.	*Gleich und gleich gesellt sich gern.*
It's enough to make a cat laugh!	*Da lachen ja die Hühner!*
The leopard can't change his spots.	*Die Katze lässt das Mausen nicht.*
Every dog has his day.	*Auch ein blindes Huhn findet mal ein Korn.*
It's raining cats and dogs.	*Es gießt wie aus Eimern.*
The early bird catches the worm.	*Morgenstund' hat Gold im Mund.*

54 ★★★

Die folgenden Sätze enthalten mit **Präpositionen verknüpfte Verben**. Markieren Sie die Präposition, die im Zusammenhang jeweils richtig ist.

a) Thomas is looking **for / after** his keys again. He keeps losing them.

b) Can't we take **apart / away** something and eat at home tonight?

c) Dad has just got **at / down to** doing the tax return. Don't disturb him!

d) Janie simply looked **on / to** when the boys got into a fight.

e) They spent hours discussing **about / (-)** possible solutions.

f) Why does he keep bringing **about / up** this issue?

g) Somebody has broken **in / into** Janice's new car and stolen her sunglasses.

h) Nobody can tell the twins **apart / off**. They look completely alike.

i) Have you put the good teacups back **in / into** the cupboard?

55 ★★★

Der Text enthält viele **feststehende Ausdrücke mit Präpositionen**. Welche davon sind falsch (f), welche sind richtig (r)? Korrigieren Sie die falschen Ausdrücke.

Ralph has always **dreamt of** *(r)* **(a)** starting a new life in another country. Now there's a **chance at** *(f) chance of* **(b)** realizing his dream. If he **succeeds with** ________ **(c)** his plan, he won't have to **worry over** ________ **(d)** money anymore. At the moment Ralph has to **rely on** ________ **(e)** his luck because he has had **difficulty with** ________ **(f)** finding a bank which **approves of** ________ **(g)** his business plan. But he has always been **good in** ________ **(h)** promoting himself and he is also quite **famous for** ________ **(i)** being an optimist. The **idea about** ________ **(j)** starting a new life will keep him going. Susie, his wife, has never been **interested at** ________ **(k)** going abroad, though. She doesn't want to **leave behind** ________ **(l)** her friends and family.

Grund- und Ordnungszahlen

56 ★

Schreiben Sie die folgenden **Zahlen** in englischen Worten auf. Die jeweils angegebenen Buchstaben ergeben zusammen ein weiteres Zahlwort.

a) 4 *four*

b) 9 ______

c) 13 ______ (5. Buchstabe)

d) 28 ______ (2. Buchstabe)

e) 18 ______ (6. Buchstabe)

f) 14 ______ (8. Buchstabe)

g) 12 ______ (1. Buchstabe)

h) 40 ______ (5. Buchstabe)

i) 55 ______ (6. Buchstabe)

j) 90 ______ (3. Buchstabe)

k) 19 ______ (2. Buchstabe)

l) 103 ______ (2. Buchstabe)

m) 69 ______ (9. Buchstabe)

n) 277 ______

Lösungswort: ______

!

Die englischen Zahlenwörter werden jeweils einzeln bzw. mit Bindestrich geschrieben, nicht wie im Deutschen zusammen, z. B.:

357 **three hundred and fifty-seven** *dreihundertsiebenundfünfzig*

57 ★

Entwirren Sie die Wortschlangen und notieren Sie die englischen Ziffern.

a) threehundredandthirty-threepointthree

333.3 ____________________

b) onethousandsevenhundredandsixtypointohfourone

____

c) twelvethousandsixhundredandseventy-fivepointseventwonine

____

d) twohundredandsixteenthousandeighthundredandfifteen

____

e) sixmillionfivehundredandforty-threethousandtwohundredandeleven

____

!

Achten Sie auf die unterschiedliche Verwendung der Interpunktion:

(0).01	= point oh one	*null Komma null eins (0,01)*
1,000	= a/one thousand	*(ein)tausend (1.000 oder 1 000)*
1,000,000	= a/one million	*eine Million (1.000.000 oder 1 000 000)*
1,000,000,000	= a/one billion	*eine Milliarde (1.000.000.000)*

58 ★★

Übertragen Sie die Begriffe ins Englische. Schreiben Sie die Zahlen aus.

a) *dreimal drei* *three times three*

b) *ein- oder zweimal* ____________________

c) *Hunderte von Leuten* ____________________

d) *ein halber Apfel* ____________________

e) *hundertmal* ____________________

f) *zwei Hälften* ______________________

g) *2½ Kilometer* ______________________

h) *eine Dreiviertelstunde* ______________________

i) *0,25 Liter* ______________________

j) *die zwölfte Stunde* ______________________

k) *die deutschen Teammitglieder belegten den 1., 2., 8. und 9. Platz*

____

In Telefonnummern wird **0** oft **[əʊ]** statt **zero** gesprochen, z. B. **zero** one double **zero** five oder **oh** one double **oh** five.

59 ★★

Ergänzen Sie die Sätze, indem Sie die richtige Möglichkeit auswählen.

a) It was too much. They only ate ...
- ☐ A a third of the cake.
- ☐ B a third cake.

b) I only met him ...
- ☐ A first.
- ☐ B once.

c) I'd like ...
- ☐ A half a watermelon, please.
- ☐ B a half watermelon, please.

d) They dug out ...
- ☐ A two hundred tons of soil.
- ☐ B two hundreds of tons of soil.

e) The earth holds more than ...
- ☐ A six milliard people.
- ☐ B six billion people.

f) He was one of the heroes of the ...
- ☐ A twentyth century.
- ☐ B twentieth century.

Datum und Uhrzeiten

60 ★★

Unser Tagesablauf besteht aus Uhrzeiten und Terminen. Wie lauten die abgebildeten **Uhrzeiten** in herkömmlicher und digitaler Ausdrucksweise?

a) *It's (a) quarter past six.*
It's six fifteen.

b) ____________________

c) ____________________

d) ____________________

e) ____________________

f) ____________________

g) ____________________

h) ____________________

61 ★★

Vervollständigen Sie die Sätze mit der jeweils richtigen **Jahreszahl**.

AD 33 ▪ from 1939 until 1945 ▪ in 2001 ▪ in the sixth century ▪
in the early and the late 70s ▪ in the year 1929 ▪
on 15th March 44 BC ▪ the roaring twenties

a) Terrorists attacked the Twin Towers ______________________.

b) Julius Cesar was murdered ______________________.

c) There was an oil crisis ______________________.

d) It is assumed that Jesus died ______________________.

e) In Europe, World War II lasted ______________________.

f) ______________________ were the time of jazz music and Art Déco.

g) There was a severe Wall Street Crash ______________________.

h) King Arthur is said to have lived ______________________.

BC = Before Christ (*vor Christi Geburt*) **AD** = Anno Domini (*nach Christi Geburt*)

Man spricht im Englischen in der Regel jedoch nur die Kurzform.

62 ★★

Wie lauten die **Datumsangaben** und **Uhrzeiten** in gesprochener Sprache?

a) July 4, 2012 ______________________

b) 3.47 p.m. ______________________

c) 23rd April 1999 ______________________

d) 8.07 a.m. ______________________

e) 11.21.13 ______________________

f) 2 May 1954 ______________________

Beachten Sie die Unterschiede bei Datumsangaben in GB und den USA, z. B.:

BE: 06.12.2015 (TT.MM.JJJJ)	the sixth of December/December the sixth, two thousand and fifteen
AE: 12.06.2015 (MM.TT.JJJJ)	December sixth, two thousand (and) fifteen

Adjektive

63 ★

Wie lauten die **Adjektive für Nationalitätszugehörigkeiten** für die folgenden Länder auf Englisch im Singular und Plural?

a) America *an American, the Americans*

b) Britain ______

c) Germany ______

d) Wales ______

e) Scotland ______

f) England ______

g) Portugal ______

h) Spain ______

i) Greece ______

j) New Zealand ______

k) The Netherlands ______

64 ★

Ergänzen Sie die Sätze mit der korrekten Auswahl.

a) I would like a bottle of mineral water, please, ...

☐ A the large one.

☐ B a large ones.

☐ C a large one.

b) You really need a new blouse. What about ...

☐ A the one?

☐ B these one?

☐ C this one?

c) Which children belong to you?

- ☐ A The young one or the one with the curls?
- ☐ B The younger ones or the ones with the curls?
- ☐ C The youngest ones or the ones with the curls?

d) Look at these flowers.

- ☐ A What ones would you prefer?
- ☐ B Which ones would you prefer?
- ☐ C Whose one would you prefer?

65 ★★

Die Satzteile ergeben je zwei Sätze, wenn Sie das Adjektiv jeweils zweimal verwenden. Achten Sie dabei auf die richtige Stellung der Adjektive.

a) your | stole | brother | your | crazy | my guinea pig | brother | is

____

b) we | the | has turned | the | milk | sour | can't drink | milk | heat

____

c) a | always | I | tells | to stay | he | am | calm | person | me

____

d) the | wonderful | bride | a | she | bride | looks | is

____

!

Drücken die Verben **look**, **smell**, **taste** und **sound** eine Tätigkeit aus, werden sie mit einem Adverb (nicht mit einem Adjektiv) verwendet, z. B.:

He tasted the steak **greedily**. *Er probierte gierig das Steak.*

66 ★★

An welchen Stellen können die **Stützwörter one** oder **ones** den Originaltext ersetzen? Schreiben Sie die Sätze entsprechend um.

a) We have a lot of books at home. Those books over there are all on Shakespeare, while these are works by Mark Twain and this is a new book on cats.

Those ones over there are ______________________

____

____

b) Which wines did you enjoy? – That sparkling white wine from Australia was excellent, but I also liked the three red wines we tasted.

____

____

____

c) I like these paintings. – Which paintings? These paintings right here or those Matisse paintings over there, or do you mean this modern painting?

____

____

____

67 ★★

Manche **Adjektive** können nur vor Substantiven, andere nur mit Verben verwendet werden. Welche der folgenden Formulierungen sind jeweils korrekt?

a) ☐ A an ill child
☐ B The child is ill.

b) ☐ A an only child
☐ B The child is only.

c) ☐ A an afraid child
☐ B The child is afraid.

d) ☐ A an asleep child
☐ B The child is asleep.

68 ★★★

Übersetzen Sie die Ausdrücke in Klammern und tragen Sie sie ein.

a) *The emotional thing* *(Das Emotionale)* about our relationship was both ________ *(wunderbar)* and ________ *(überwältigend)*.

b) ________ *(die jungen Leute)* and ________ *(die älteren Leute)* cannot always understand each other.

c) ________ *(Behinderte)* often have problems with ________ *(dem Alltäglichen)*.

d) ________ *(Das Gute)* about this flat is its garden, but ________ *(das Schlechte)* about it is its expensive heating.

e) Movies of the 1950s often go for ________ *(das Melodramatische)*.

f) As ________ *(behinderter Mensch)* one often has to fight misconceptions.

Present participles und **past participles** können auch als Adjektive verwendet werden, z. B.:

Barking dogs seldom bite.	*Bellende Hunde ...*
You can't withdraw money from a **frozen** account.	*... gesperrten Konto.*

Adverbien

69 ★

Welche der Wörter sind **Adverbien**? Markieren Sie sie.

always deadly extremely famously fantastically funky
heavy lucky nice often old quick quietly
silly simply still today

!

Manche Adverbien sind unregelmäßig und haben z. B. die gleiche Form wie das Adjektiv. Man muss sie auswendig lernen!

You're driving **fast**. (≠ fastly)
I arrived home **late**. (≠ lately)

John has to work **hard**. (≠ hardly)
Mary has researched **well**. (≠ goodly)

Aber: My aunt is **well**. (≠ good) *Meiner Tante geht es gesundheitlich gut.*

70 ★

Finden Sie die Adjektive im Text und bilden Sie das entsprechende Adverb. Achten Sie dabei auf Ausnahmen bei der Bildung!

Timmy is quite a shy boy. He is good at school and although he works hard at the weekends he is never late on Mondays. Sometimes he worries about saving enough money for his fees. Nevertheless he is full of plans for his new life at university. Though he is quite sure that the start will be terrible for him, he thinks he will be happy there eventually and have a fantastic time.

Adjectives	Adverbs

71
★★

Ordnen Sie die Sätze, sodass die **Adverbien der unbestimmten Zeit und Häufigkeit** an der jeweils richtigen Stelle im Satz stehen.

a) always | wash | do | your hair | you | in the shower | ?

____

b) getting up | usually | like | I | in the morning | .

____

c) home | gets | never | he | before | 7 p.m. | .

____

d) seldom | I | my keys | find | can | .

____

e) not always | have | I | a bath | do | .

____

f) don't | I | to | normally | work | walk | .

____

g) bored | she | sometimes | with her job | is | .

____

!

Adverbien der unbestimmten Zeit und Häufigkeit stehen

- vor dem Verb: She **often forgets** her wallet.
- nach **be** als Vollverb: She **is usually** a very organized person.
- nach dem 1. Hilfsverb: But she **would never** forget her sunglasses.

Adverbien der bestimmten Zeit, wie z. B. **today**, **last Sunday**, stehen am Satzanfang oder -ende.

Adverbien der bestimmten Häufigkeit, wie z. B. **daily**, **twice a month**, stehen dagegen am Satzende.

72 ★★

Achtung Glatteis: Welche der Wörter sind **Adverbien** und welche **Adjektive**, welche sind beides? Schreiben Sie den jeweils zugehörigen adverbialen Ausdruck bzw. das Adjektiv in die Spalte ganz rechts.

	Adjektiv	Adverb	zugehöriges Adverb/Adjektiv
a) friendly	☒	☐	*in a friendly way/manner*
b) lively	☐	☐	
c) kindly	☐	☐	
d) deadly	☐	☐	
e) early	☐	☐	
f) silly	☐	☐	
g) lonely	☐	☐	
h) daily	☐	☐	
i) rudely	☐	☐	
j) cowardly	☐	☐	
k) lovely	☐	☐	

73 ★★

Bilden Sie aus den vorgegebenen Wörtern die jeweils passenden **Adjektive** oder **Adverbien** und bringen Sie sie in die richtige Reihenfolge.

a) George can play the saxophone ______________________ (good, very).

b) I think this job is ______________________ (paid, bad).

c) **Jane:** How ______________________ (good) can you speak French?

Carlo: ______________________ (good, very).

d) I arrived at the station ______________________ (late, too) to catch the bus.

e) Your hair looks ______________________ (nice, styled).

f) Leo has become ______________________ (fair, independent).

g) Rex is ______________________ (quite, usual, friendly).

h) My sister is still ______________________ (offended, deep).

i) Our neighbour has insulted her ______________________ (horrible).

j) He behaved ______________________ (rude, late, very).

k) She'll ______________________ (never, certain, almost) forgive him.

l) We all can understand her ______________________ (good, quite).

74

★★★

Oft gibt es mehrere Möglichkeiten, etwas auszudrücken. Wandeln Sie die folgenden Sätze um und verwenden Sie statt des **Adjektivs** ein **Adverb**.

a) My mum is a bad driver. *My mum/She drives badly.*

b) Antonia is a very good rider. ______________________

c) Mr Clemens is a brilliant teacher. ______________________

d) Tom is a competent yoga instructor. ______________________

e) My cousin is a passionate painter. ______________________

f) Wolfgang is an avid sailor. ______________________

g) Angie is an ingenious gardener. ______________________

h) José is a fantastic guitar player. ______________________

i) Anne is an imaginative writer. ______________________

75 ★★★

Können Sie die verschiedenen **Adverbien** richtig in die Sätze einfügen? Manchmal gibt es mehrere Möglichkeiten.

a) Marcie visited us. (fortunately, last weekend)

b) She enjoys her visits. (here, usually)

c) She spoke with us. (this time, really, never)

d) We found out what was troubling her. (all the time, finally)

e) She had lost Grandma's watch. (outside, apparently, somewhere)

f) It turned out she had left it in her gym locker. (the weekend before, simply)

g) She is going to look after the watch. (very, now, carefully)

h) We lost our keys. (twice, unfortunately, last month)

!

Für mehrere Adverbien am Satzende gilt die Regel „Art und Weise vor Ort vor Zeit" (**manner** – **place** – **time**), wobei genauere vor allgemeineren Zeitangaben stehen. Ausnahme: Adverbiale Bestimmungen des Mittels stehen zwischen Orts- und Zeitangabe, z. B.:

Luckily Lara drove me **quickly to the station by car last Monday**.

Steigerungsformen und Vergleiche

76 ★

Ergänzen Sie die in der Tabelle fehlenden Formen.

	Grundform	Komparativ	Superlativ
a)	hot		
b)			furthest
c)		simpler	
d)	much		
e)			happiest
f)		stronger	
g)	nice		
h)		less	

Vor Verwandtschaftsbeziehungen stehen statt **older/oldest** oft die Formen **elder/eldest**. Achtung: **Elder/Eldest** werden nicht in Verbindung mit **than** verwendet!

My **elder sister** is **older than** Carol. *Meine <u>ältere</u> Schwester ist <u>älter</u> als Carol.*

77 ★

Wie lauten die **Steigerungsformen** folgender Adverbien?

a) early *earlier – earliest*

b) stupidly ____________

c) often ____________

d) happily ____________

e) hard ____________

f) slowly ____________

78 ★★

Schreiben Sie die passende englische **Vergleichsform** in die Lücke.

a) Ben Nevis is ______ *(höher als)* Snowdon.

b) My brother is ______ *(dünner als)* I am.

c) This book is ______ *(so gut wie)* the film.

d) Is Rubens ______ *(berühmter als)* van Dyck?

e) Gerry is ______ *(beschäftigter als)* George.

f) Swimming is ______ *(nicht so interessant wie)* walking.

g) Physics can be ______ *(anspruchsvoller als)* PE.

79 ★★

Bilden Sie die **Superlative** und vervollständigen Sie damit die Sätze.

bad • big • dangerous • good • interesting • lazy • much/many • narrow • near • small

a) John is the ______ person in the family. Everybody else is small.

b) Fido is definitely the ______ dog in the world! He sleeps all day.

c) What's the ______ way to get to the town hall? I have no map.

d) Where can I find the ______ museum?

e) Jacob is the ______ player in the football club. He's so slow.

f) He's so irritable – the ______ cause will drive him up the wall.

g) The ______ steaks you will get in Canada.

h) It's great weather! Let's make the ______ of the day and go out.

i) I believe the ______ alleys can be found in Italy.

j) Some people love doing the ______ sports in the world.

80 ★★

Wie werden hier die **Stützwörter** richtig angewendet? Wählen Sie aus.

a) Which shoes would you prefer? –

I prefer ...

☐ A the more elegant ones.

☐ B the more elegant one.

☐ C the eleganter ones.

b) What kind of holiday do you like? –

We like ...

☐ A the warmly kind.

☐ B the more warm kinds.

☐ C the warmer kind.

c) What type of house do you plan to buy? –

We plan to buy ...

☐ A the impressiver one.

☐ B one of the more impressive type.

☐ C the impressively type.

d) What sort of problem did you have with your car? –

I had ...

☐ A the steamyer sort.

☐ B the more steamy sort.

☐ C one of the steamier sort.

81

Die Sätze sind durcheinandergeraten. Wie lauten sie richtig?

★★

a) them | two | the | the | the | of | get | sooner | , | better | married | !

____

b) news | on | the | as | she | turned | hearing | as | a | white | sheet | .

____

c) sister | is | elder | than | a | head | my | older | three | taller | and | years | me | .

____

d) faster | antelope | run | fastest | than | the | !

____

Für Vergleiche, die im Deutschen mit „je ... desto ..." formuliert werden, verwendet man im Englischen die Formulierung **the** + **comparative ... the** + **comparative ...**:

The hotter it gets, **the more** one should drink.
Je heißer es wird, desto mehr sollte man trinken.

82

Übersetzen Sie.

★★

a) *Marie spielt besser Geige als Lisa, aber Lisa ist die Netteste in der Gruppe.*

____

b) *Kannst du mir bitte die Schüssel da reichen – Welche? Die kleinere oder die größere?*

____

____

c) *Calvin weiß nicht weniger über Dinosaurier als Susie, obwohl sie sonst immer die Schlaueste ist.* ______________________________

____

d) *Tom kann nicht so schnell schwimmen wie Jerry. Aber er kann viel weiter springen als Jerry.* ______________________________

____

83 ★★★

Wie lautet jeweils das **Adjektiv**? Tragen Sie es in das Kreuzworträtsel ein.
Achtung: Manchmal werden Ausweichformen benötigt!

a) most often
b) very speedily
c) the earliest
d) more clearly
e) in the least
f) more automatically
g) the furthest
h) in the friendliest way
i) lately
j) cleverest
k) wholly
l) most truly

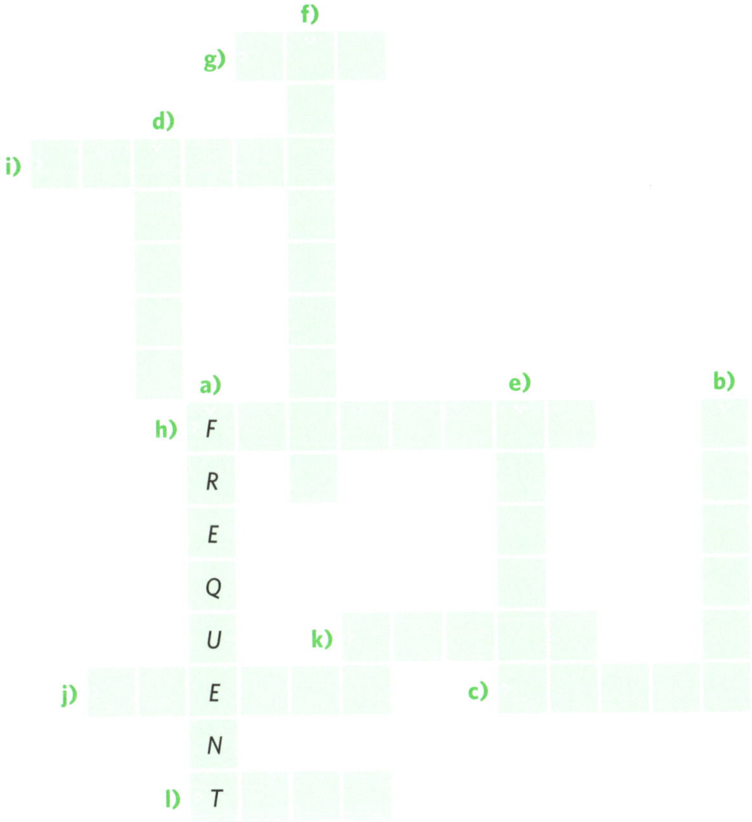

Verbformen und Imperativ

84 ★

Notieren Sie den **Infinitiv** und bilden Sie dann das **present participle** der Verben, die auf den Fotos dargestellt sind.

a) *whisper,* *whispering*

b) ______

c) ______

d) ______

e) ______

f) ______

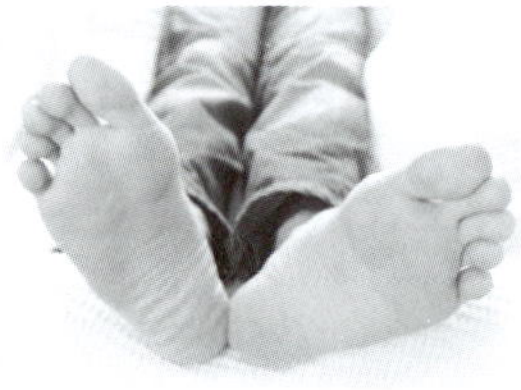

g) ______

h) ______

i) ______

ABC

Das Verb **drive** + Transportmittel (z. B. **a bus**, **a car**) bedeutet stets, dass man selbst fährt!

I love **driving my new car**. *Ich liebe es, mein neues Auto zu fahren.*

85 ★

Hinter diesen Buchstabensalaten verbergen sich verschiedene **Verbformen (past simple, past participle, present participle)**. Schreiben Sie sie auf und notieren sie den Namen der jeweiligen Verbform.

	Verb	Bezeichnung der Verbform
a) wnosh	*shown*	*past participle*
b) kadrn	______	______
c) gilokon	______	______
d) schoen	______	______
e) urn	______	______
f) gintirw	______	______
g) tea	______	______

86 ★

Partizipien können auch als Adjektive gebraucht werden. Entscheiden Sie, ob das **present** oder **past participle** jeweils passt und tragen Sie es ein.

a) It's important not to wake the *sleeping* (sleep) children.

b) They were talking about the matter behind ______ (close) doors.

c) I shut the window because of the ______ (bark) dogs.

d) The electronic media and the ______ (print) word are called the 'rivals of the modern age'.

e) My colleagues told me about the ______ (shock) incident.

f) We were devastated when we saw the ______ (damage) house.

g) Our daughter is dreaming of a ______ (fly) carpet for herself.

h) Luckily, the ______ (forget) documents weren't necessary.

87 ★★

Bringen Sie die Bruchstücke dieser **Aufforderungen** in die richtige Reihenfolge. Manchmal gibt es zwei Möglichkeiten.

a) door | shut | please | the | , | .

b) tell | Josie | to | don't | to | call | forget | Mum | .

c) when | the mixer | start | never | open | it | is | .

d) not | walk | do | the lawn | on | please | .

e) not | let's | to | go | that party | .

f) this | let's | to | our | Spain | holiday | go | for | year | .

g) don't | drink | and | drive | .

h) take | and | make | a seat | yourself | comfortable | .

i) do | time | lunch | be | in | back | for | .

!

Aufforderungen enden im Englischen grundsätzlich mit einem Punkt. Nur bei besonders betonten Befehlen setzt man ein Ausrufezeichen.

88 ★★

Welche der folgenden Verbformen muss hier jeweils eingesetzt werden: **infinitive**, **present participle**, **past simple** oder **past participle**?

a) She ______________ *(arbeiten)* in a restaurant a few years ago.

b) He has just had his hair ______________ *(schneiden)*.

c) The car was almost brand-new when it was ______________ *(stehlen)*.

d) I used to ______________ *(spielen)* the guitar regularly.

e) You can ______________ *(werfen)* the paper away – I've read it.

f) The river remained ______________ *(schließen)* for shipping for weeks because of high water.

g) My sister is ______________ *(reisen)* through Mexico right now.

h) Joe has never ______________ *(nachdenken)* about looking for another job.

i) Jennifer would ______________ *(nähen)* the skirt herself if she had time.

j) My mum always tells me ______________ *(sein)* careful.

k) Todd lay ______________ *(dösen)* in the sun for hours and got a sunburn.

l) Mrs Carstairs noticed the burglars ______________ *(durchstreifen)* her garden in time to ______________ *(anrufen)* the police.

m) ______________ *(reisen)* requires time, money and good nerves.

n) Last weekend we ______________ *(gehen)* to the cinema and afterwards we ______________ *(sein)* in a nice bar.

o) People are ______________ *(scherzen)* that ______________ *(segeln)* is equivalent to ______________ *(nehmen)* a cold shower and ______________ *(zerreißen)* £50 notes at the same time.

Ob ein **gerund** oder ein **infinitive** nach einem Verb folgt, lässt sich nicht aus der deutschen Übersetzung ableiten. Die Wendungen muss man einfach lernen.

89 ★★

Vervollständigen Sie die Sätze, indem Sie das korrekte Satzende wählen. Manchmal gibt es mehrere Möglichkeiten.

a) Yesterday I watched our neighbour ...

- ☐ **A** mowing and watering the lawn.
- ☐ **B** mow and water the lawn.

b) He noticed me standing there and asked me ...

- ☐ **A** what do against his mossy lawn.
- ☐ **B** what to do against his mossy lawn.

c) I warned him ...

- ☐ **A** to not over-fertilize his lawn.
- ☐ **B** not to over-fertilize his lawn.

d) He made me ...

- ☐ **A** coming over and look at the lawn more closely.
- ☐ **B** come over and look at the lawn more closely.

e) I told him I would ...

- ☐ **A** try to break up the soil a bit.
- ☐ **B** trying to break up the soil a bit.

f) He should go to a garden centre ...

- ☐ **A** to borrow a machine for pulling up all that moss.
- ☐ **B** in order to borrow a machine for pulling up all that moss.

90 ★★★

Ersetzen Sie die Relativsätze durch ein jeweils passendes **Partizip**. Achtung: Das funktioniert nicht immer!

a) The book which was ordered last week hasn't come yet.

The book ordered last week hasn't come yet.

b) Bosses who openly complain about their employees aren't popular.

______

c) I don't know the man who asked me after your address.

______

d) She's got a date with the boy that she met in the cinema last week.

______

e) People that don't smile when you meet them are disagreeable.

______

f) The house that was sold in our street has been torn down.

______

g) Most cats that live in the house want to sleep in their owners' beds.

______

ABC

a date

1. Zeitangabe, Datum
2. Verabredung mit Freund(in)

What's your date of birth?
Wie ist dein/Ihr Geburtsdatum?

Who is your date?
Mit wem bist du verabredet?

data (+ Verb im Singular)

wissenschaftliche Daten

The data has been processed.
Die Daten sind verarbeitet worden.

Data abuse is a common offence.
Datenmissbrauch ist ein häufiges Vergehen.

91 ★★★

Verbinden Sie die Sätze mithilfe von **present** oder **past participles**. Achtung: Die Partizipien können ein eigenes Sinnsubjekt haben und in Verbindung mit Konjunktionen auftreten.

a) Last year we went to Wales. We had planned to go on a hiking tour there.

Having planned to go on a hiking tour there, we went to Wales last year.

b) When we drove into the mountains, we were surprised by bad weather.

______

______

c) We were blinded by the snow. Therefore we missed the turning to our B&B.

______

______

d) Finally we were found by a local. Although he knew the way, we still had problems to get to our B&B.

______

______

e) While we were drinking a grog, our dog was taking a hot bath.

______

Be, have und *do* und Modalverben

92 ★

Wie lautet jeweils die **present simple-Form** von **be, have** oder **do**?

a) They ______ (have) two dogs.

b) You ______ (be) from Maine.

c) I ______ (be) 40 years old.

d) She ______ (have) a child.

e) We ______ (be) in Bath.

f) It ______ (be) my place of birth.

g) He ______ (do) his best.

h) I always ______ (do) the dishes.

93 ★

Notieren Sie die **Kurzformen**. Manchmal gibt es mehrere Möglichkeiten.

a) I am *I'm*

b) they are ______

c) we have ______

d) she is ______

e) he does not ______

f) they did not ______

g) she was not ______

h) they were not ______

i) you are not ______

j) she has not ______

k) he has ______

l) you do not ______

94 ★

Wie lauten die **Langformen**? Ordnen Sie sie dann den passenden Personalpronomen zu. Achtung: Einige Lösungen sind austauschbar.

a) doesn't ______

b) aren't ______

c) 'm ______

d) won't ______

e) 's been ______

f) 've ______

g) 'd be ______

h) didn't ______

___ A I/you/we/you/they

___ B I/you/he/she/it/we/you/they

___ C I/you/he/she/it/we/you/they

___ D he/she/it

___ E I/you/he/she/it/we/you/they

___ F he/she/it

___ G I

___ H you/we/you/they

!

Das englische **will** entspricht nicht dem deutschen „wollen" (= **want to**):

I **will** make a dessert for the party. — *Ich mache ein Dessert für die Party.*

I **want to** make a dessert for the party. — *Ich möchte/will ein Dessert für die Party machen.*

95 ★

Übersetzen Sie die Verben ins Englische und tragen Sie sie ins Kreuzworträtsel ein. Bei verneinten Formen verwenden Sie möglichst die Kurzform. Berücksichtigen Sie auch die Apostrophe.

a) *sollen*
b) *können*
c) *müssen*
d) *brauchen*
e) *dürfen*
f) *werden*
g) *sollen nicht*
h) *nicht können*
i) *nicht müssen*
j) *nicht brauchen*
k) *nicht dürfen*
l) *werden nicht*

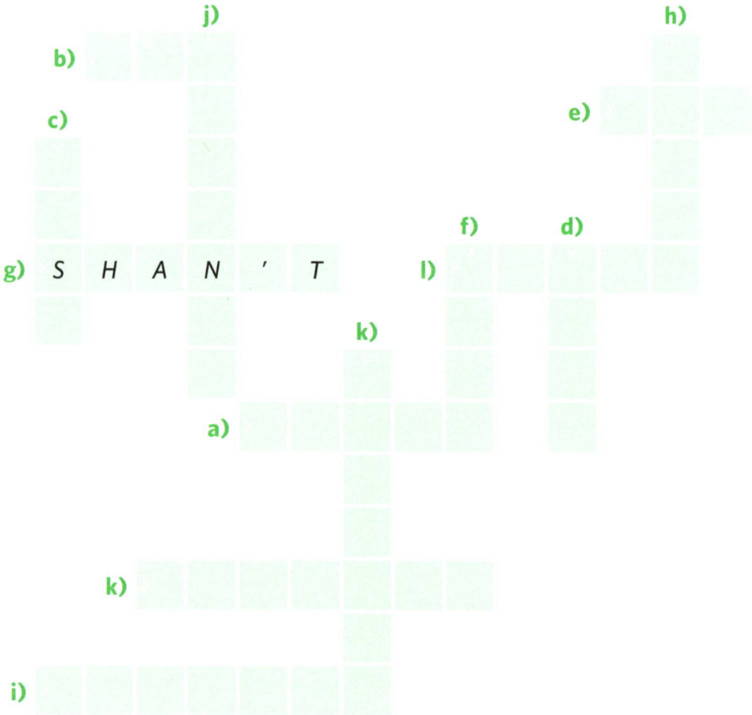

!

must not/mustn't ≠ *nicht müssen* **need not/needn't** = *nicht müssen*
Must I, Miss Sophie? – Yes, you must. / No, you **needn't**.

must not/mustn't = *nicht dürfen*
You **mustn't** disturb them now. They are studying for an exam.

96 ★

Entscheiden Sie sich für das jeweils am besten passende **Modalverb**.

a) You **can't / mustn't / needn't** ask Dad how the new washing machine works. He never goes near one.

b) Tell Lucy she **mustn't / can't / won't** walk home on her own. It will be dark and it's a lonely street.

c) The children **won't / can't / may not** eat chocolate right before lunch.

d) Sorry, but I **may / will / must** go now. My train won't wait.

e) She **may / shall / can** play the guitar at the birthday party. Everybody will love to listen to her.

f) You **can / may / must** have the paper. I've read it.

g) I **shan't / can't / won't** see anything. Are you sure there's a spot on that tie?

97 ★

Die Sätze enthalten **Modalverben** bzw. deren **Ersatzformen** in verschiedenen Zeitformen. Kreuzen Sie an, welche Zeitform jeweils verwendet wurde.

	present simple	past simple	present perfect
a) He wasn't allowed to leave.	☐	☐	☐
b) They don't have to be quiet.	☐	☐	☐
c) You shouldn't have called so late.	☐	☐	☐
d) I was going to help her that minute.	☐	☐	☐
e) She hasn't been able to help me.	☐	☐	☐
f) You're not supposed to eat sweets.	☐	☐	☐
g) Shall I bring something to eat?	☐	☐	☐

98 ★★

Geben Sie **negative Kurzantworten** auf die folgenden Fragen.

a) Will Jack have to repeat the course? *No, he won't.*

b) Have they had time to swim? ______

c) Didn't he have to pay for the damage? ______

d) May Jenny go out with us tonight? ______

e) Could the doctor help him? ______

f) Won't you be able to repair the roof? ______

g) Has Susie been allowed to come yet? ______

h) Was she allowed to come last year? ______

i) Does it have to be pork again? ______

j) Must I really eat the bread soup? ______

k) Need I bring something? ______

l) Did they do the dishes as I told them? ______

m) Am I not the luckiest guy on earth? ______

Langformen verwendet man normalerweise in der Schriftsprache oder um eine Aussage besonders zu betonen. Bei Verneinungen liegt die Betonung dann auf **not**:

I'm awful at painting. – No, you're **not**! (nicht: aren't)

99 ★★

Welche **Modal- und Ersatzformen** verstecken sich in der Wortschlange?

wollwouldbeallowedtohavhasntbeensupposedtowashadbewillhavetoshashould

______

100 ★★

Achtung Glatteis: Finden Sie die grammatikalisch korrekten Sätze. Es gibt jeweils mindestens einen korrekten Satz.

a)
☐ A Does she have a car?
☐ B Does she had a car?
☐ C Has she got a car?

b)
☐ A It was been a nice day.
☐ B It has been a nice day.
☐ C It has being a nice day.

c)
☐ A We're being silly.
☐ B We've been silly.
☐ C We're been silly.

d)
☐ A Did you had lunch?
☐ B Did you have lunch?
☐ C Do you had lunch?

Will man eine Aussage besonders betonen, kann man **do/does** vor das Vollverb setzen:

She **does** speak English very well! *Sie spricht wirklich sehr gut Englisch!*

Achtung: Das funktioniert nur bei bejahten Sätzen!

101 ★★

Welches **Modalverb** gehört zu welcher **Ersatzform** und wie heißt die Zeitform, in der diese steht?

a) must	____	A were able to	____
b) needn't	____	B is not allowed to	____
c) will	____	C had been allowed to	____
d) mustn't	____	D will not have to	____
e) can	*a)*	E has had to	*present perfect simple*
f) should	____	F would be going to	____
g) may	____	G has been supposed to	____

102 ★★★

Eine Haushaltskonferenz wird abgehalten. Wie lauten die vorgegebenen **Verben**, **Modalverben** oder **Ersatzformen** auf Englisch?

a) We ______________________ *(wollen)* help you with the housework today.

b) Josie and Josh ______________________ *(können)* do the washing up.

c) Perhaps Emma ______________________ *(würde lieber)* dust the furniture.

d) Jacob, ______________________ *(könntest du nicht)* clean the kitchen?

e) I ______________________ *(möchte gern)* lay the table.

f) ______________________ *(Müssen wir)* vacuum the living room, too?

g) Last week I ______________________ *(hatte vor)* clean the windows, but it started to rain.

h) ______________________ *(Wirst du können)* clean them today?

i) Someone ______________________ *(sollte dringend)* clean the attic as well. It's awfully dirty.

j) Who ______________________ *(sollte)* do it last time?

k) I'm not sure, but it ______________________ *(könnte vielleicht gewesen sein)* Nick's job.

l) When ______________________ *(werden wir dürfen)* stop?

– When all the work ______________________ *(erledigt sein wird)*.

ABC

Je nachdem, was man ausdrücken möchte, kann das deutsche „sollen" mit weiteren Begriffen ins Englische übersetzt werden:

be to = *sollen* (Auftrag, Vereinbarung)
Little Clara **is to** tidy up her room.

be said to/supposed to = *angeblich sollen*
Malcolm **is said to** have a girlfriend.

103 ★★★

Können Sie die Wörter in die richtige Reihenfolge bringen? Achtung: Manche Verben treten als **Modal-** und als **Vollverben** auf.

a) go | really | did | to | have | he | ?

____

b) stay | he | any | could | not | longer | .

____

c) he | could | he | waited | had | as long as | .

____

d) in | got | he | has | a hurry | or | he | is | time | ?

____

e) that dog | I | to | not | dare | would | go | near | .

____

f) not | you | about | need | him | worry | .

____

g) take | without | my car | dare | how | you | asking | !

____

h) to | shopping | we | go | need | at the weekend | .

____

i) doing | cooking | were | you | when | your homework | I | was | not | ?

____

j) you | had | time | have | to | read | longer | the | or | need | report | you | do | ?

____

____

104 ★★★

Um welche Zeitformen von **Ersatzformen** handelt es sich hier? Geben Sie sie an und auch, welches englische Modalverb dahintersteckt.

a) have been able to *present perfect simple: can*

b) was going to ______

c) will have had to ______

d) would be supposed to ______

e) has been allowed to ______

f) would have been able to ______

g) won't have to ______

h) hadn't been allowed to ______

Denken Sie daran, dass Fragen oder Äußerungen mit **would like to** höflicher sind als mit **want to**:

I'**d like to** go out for dinner.
Ich würde gerne zum Abendessen ausgehen.

I **want to** go into that boutique there.
Ich will in die Boutique da gehen.

105 ★★★

Welche Sätze enthalten **be**, **have** oder **do** als Vollverb, welche als Hilfsverb? Kreuzen Sie an.

	Hilfsverb	Vollverb
a) Our neighbour Jean is from France.	☐	☐
b) He has a wonderful old cabriolet.	☐	☐
c) He's been looking for it for a long time.	☐	☐
d) He was dreaming of a light-blue one.	☐	☐
e) But he didn't want it to be too expensive.	☐	☐
f) Now he would do everything to keep it safe.	☐	☐

106

★★★

Bilden Sie mit den Verben jeweils die angegebene Zeitform.

a) can do	past simple	*was/were able to do*
b) may have	present perfect simple	
c) be	past perfect simple	
d) must be	future simple	
e) have	conditional perfect simple	
f) mustn't have	present perfect simple	
g) need to do	present simple	
h) do	future perfect simple	
i) dare to be	conditional simple	
j) needn't do	past perfect simple	

107

★★★

Übersetzen Sie ins Englische. Achten Sie auf die **Modalverben**.

a) *Ich möchte wissen, wo Pete steckt.*

b) *Er muss das Flugzeug verpasst haben.*

c) *Es könnte sein, dass er immer noch am Flughafen wartet.*

d) *Er hätte nicht so spät losfahren sollen.*

e) *Warum kann er nie pünktlich sein?*

Gerundien und Infinitive

108 ★

Üben Sie die ***ing*-Formen**, indem Sie in den folgenden Sätzen die jeweils richtige Form in die Lücke schreiben.

a) Jane enjoys *going skiing* (go skiing).

b) Do you like ________________ (read)?

c) Bert dislikes ________________ (jog).

d) Our dog loves ________________ (run).

e) Fiona likes ________________ (have) lots of clocks.

f) Our cat doesn't like ________________ (be) left alone.

g) I hate ________________ (do) the dishes.

Ein **gerund** steht meistens nach Verben, die eine <u>Abneigung</u> oder eine <u>Vorliebe</u> ausdrücken, z. B. **love**, **hate**, **like**, **dislike**, **prefer**, **enjoy**, **can't stand**, **(don't) mind**.

109 ★

Entscheiden Sie, welche der Sätze ein **gerund** enthalten (und welche eine andere Art *ing*-Form).

	gerund: **yes**	**no**
a) Joe is going to stay on his uncle's farm all summer.	☐	☐
b) Joe likes riding very much.	☐	☐
c) Other sports are boring in his opinion.	☐	☐
d) Joe learns fascinating things about horses on the farm.	☐	☐
e) Helping in the stable is fun, Joe thinks.	☐	☐
f) Joe's other favourite occupation is caring for the horses.	☐	☐
g) He'll soon be very good at working with horses.	☐	☐

110 ★

In diesen Buchstabensalaten sind **gerunds** versteckt. Aus den bezeichneten Buchstaben der Lösungswörter ergibt sich ein weiteres **gerund**.

a) arginriv ______________ (1. und 2. Buchstabe)

b) getgfortin ______________ (4. Buchstabe)

c) ignotcinnu ______________ (7. Buchstabe)

d) oingpen ______________ (5., 6. und 7. Buchstabe)

Lösung: ______________

111 ★

Bringen Sie die Satzteile in die richtige Reihenfolge und entscheiden Sie, ob das **gerund** bzw. der **infinitive** jeweils Subjekt (S) oder Objekt (O) ist.

a) can | risky | new recipes | be | cooking | .

Cooking new recipes can be risky. (S)

b) like | my brother's | friends | of | some | wrestling | .

____

c) is | very important | for | training | a good sportsman or -woman | .

____

d) likes | Max | a lot | to eat | .

____

e) on holiday | dozens of postcards | to write | is | rather | stressful | .

____

f) with | a bride's gown | tiring | your mother | can be | choosing | .

____

112 ★★

Die Satzanfänge lassen sich jeweils mit zwei der angebotenen Lösungen korrekt vervollständigen. Welche sind das?

a) I have no idea ...

- ☐ A which way to go.
- ☐ B which way I have to go.
- ☐ C which way going.

b) My cousin was the first of us ...

- ☐ A learning scuba-diving.
- ☐ B to learn scuba-diving.
- ☐ C who learnt scuba-diving.

c) He worked hard ...

- ☐ A for achieving his goal.
- ☐ B so that he would achieve his goal.
- ☐ C to achieve his goal.

d) He was the youngest scuba-diver ...

- ☐ A that explored the Devil's Table.
- ☐ B explore the Devil's Table.
- ☐ C to explore the Devil's Table.

113 ★★

Steht nach diesen Verben ein **gerund** (G) oder ein **infinitive** (I)?

a) decide + I
b) suggest + ___
c) finish + ___
d) plan + ___
e) learn + ___
f) go + ___
g) promise + ___
h) practise + ___
i) enjoy + ___
j) hope + ___
k) offer + ___
l) agree + ___
m) go on + ___
n) be sorry + ___
o) be interested in + ___
p) refuse + ___
q) be afraid of + ___
r) look forward to + ___

114

★★

Können hier **gerund**, **infinitive** oder beides stehen?

a) I'm sorry **missing / to miss** your party.

b) Jeannie is always afraid **losing / to lose** her wallet or her keys.

c) The kids would like **going / to go** to the zoo next Saturday.

d) Emma is still worrying about **failing / to fail** her exam.

e) The dustbin lorry starts **emptying / to empty** the bins terribly early.

f) Martin likes **driving / to drive** fast.

g) I can't stand **sleeping / to sleep** in the car.

115

★★

Der **infinitive** kann Relativsätze und andere Nebensätze ersetzen. Formen Sie die folgenden Sätze um, indem Sie einen **infinitive** verwenden.

a) I was offered several dresses which I could try on.

I was offered several dresses to try on.

b) A horror movie isn't something you should watch before you go to bed.

____

c) There's a special code which you must enter if you want to open the door.

____

d) Sam told me the job which might have suited her had been given to Jess.

____

e) The best time when a problem should be handled is not always the earliest.

____

Werden Verb + Infinitiv ins Deutsche übersetzt, wird das **to** meist mit „zu" übersetzt:

I'm afraid **to** lose my keys.	*Ich habe Angst, meine Schlüssel <u>zu</u> verlieren.*
She hoped **to** finish her exam soon.	*Sie hoffte, ihre Prüfung bald <u>abzuschließen</u>.*

116 ★★

Wann steht der **infinitive** mit **to**, wann ohne **to**? Tragen Sie die jeweils passenden Satzanfänge ein. Manchmal gibt es mehrere Möglichkeiten.

All neighbours watched my house • I asked my neighbour • Dad warned me • He told them • The witness saw the thief • My neighbour noticed two men • Grandma heard me • Mom advised me

a) ______________________ get up in the night.

b) ______________________ go into the bank.

c) ______________________ to go on a long holiday.

d) ______________________ not to leave my house unattended.

e) ______________________ to look after my house during my holiday.

f) ______________________ prowl around the house.

g) ______________________ to disappear or wait for the police.

h) ______________________ to prevent a break-in then.

Verben des Ratens, Aufforderns oder Warnens stehen mit Objekt und **infinitive** + **to**.

Verben des Wahrnehmens und Beobachtens stehen mit Objekt und **infinitive without to**. Der **infinitive without to** folgt außerdem nach den meisten Modalverben, Verben wie z. B. **make**, **let** und nach Ausdrücken wie **I would rather .../I had better ...**

I **should go** home.
You **made me eat** too much.
I **would rather stay** than go.

117 ★★

Ergänzen Sie die Sätze, indem Sie **Verb** und **Verneinung(en)** richtig einsetzen.

a) She (not promise, **past simple**; talk, **infinitive**) about this matter.

She didn't promise to talk about this matter.

b) She (promise, **past simple**; not talk, **infinitive**) about this matter.

____

c) She (not promise, **past simple**; not talk, **infinitive**) about this matter.

____

d) They (be prepared, **present simple**; not talk, **infinitive**) about the issue.

____

e) They (not be prepared, **present simple**; talk, **infinitive**) about the issue.

____

118 ★★★

Ergänzen Sie die folgenden Sätze, so dass sie einen **infinitive** enthalten (z. B. eine Passivform, eine Verlaufsform oder eine Perfektform).

a) Somebody should have watered the lawn.

→ The lawn should ______________________.

b) It also needs mowing.

→ It also needs ______________________.

c) Look at that! It seems our neighbour's garden is being redesigned at last.

→ Our neighbour seems ______________________.

d) Can he repair that fence?

→ Yes, the fence can ______________________.

119 ★★★

Achtung Glatteis: Nach welchen dieser teilweise sehr ähnlichen Ausdrücke steht das **gerund**, nach welchen der **infinitive**?

a) It's no good ____________ (ask) for cherries in December.

b) It's worth ____________ (try) to solve the problem.

c) It's important ____________ (keep) all doors locked at night.

d) It's not very useful ____________ (start) the wash without detergent.

e) It's unusual for him ____________ (come) home so late.

f) It's no use ____________ (complain) about the price of fuel.

g) There's no ____________ (know) what might happen in the future.

h) It's not good ____________ (keep) the cats indoors for too long.

i) It's a pity for that nice house not ____________ (be) occupied.

120 ★★★

Nach einigen Verben kann sowohl ein **gerund** als auch ein **infinitive** stehen. Allerdings gibt es Bedeutungsunterschiede. Übersetzen Sie.

a) I stopped listening to the radio when the phone rang.

____

b) I stopped to pick up my mother from the hairdresser's.

____

c) She remembered to buy stamps when she walked past the post office.

____

d) She remembered taking out her wallet at the post office.

____

e) Did I forget to put my wallet back into my handbag?

____

f) I forgot putting my wallet into the glove compartment instead of my bag.

____

g) The rabbits tried to break out, but they didn't try digging a tunnel.

____

Ein Bedeutungsunterschied zwischen **infinitive** und **gerund** besteht nach:

regret + infinitive – Zukünftiges
mean + infinitive – Absicht

regret + gerund – Vergangenes
mean + gerund – Folge

Achtung: Bei den Verben **begin**, **continue**, **start**, **hate**, **like**, **love** und **prefer** gibt es praktisch keinen Bedeutungsunterschied zwischen den Konstruktionen mit Infinitiv oder Gerundium.

121 ★★★

Gerund oder **infinitive**? Bilden Sie die korrekte Form des Verbs und des jeweiligen Sinnsubjekts.

a) My sister is afraid of ______________ (I, tell) stories about her boyfriend.

b) I didn't expect ______________ (you, arrive) so early.

c) Do you mind ______________ (I, close) the windows?

d) Would you like ______________ (I, pick) you up after our appointment?

e) Maya wants ______________ (Chris, watch) romantic films with her.

f) Have you heard about ______________ (Carol, get) a place at Harvard?

ABC

purse	*Geldbörse* (BE); *Handtasche* (AE)
wallet	*Brieftasche; Dokumentenmappe* (BE)
briefcase	*Aktentasche*
handbag	*Handtasche* (BE)

Present simple und progressive

122 ★

Welche Verbform des **present simple** ist richtig? Wählen Sie je eine aus.

Tom work / works / worked **(a)** as a fireman. Before he goes / go / going **(b)** to work in the morning he buy / buys / bought **(c)** himself a large coffee. When you ask / asks / asked **(d)** him about his job, he explain / explained / explains **(e)** it can / could **(f)** be dangerous sometimes. But he and his colleagues do / did / does **(g)** not have exciting days very often. They reads / read **(h)** the paper and watch / watched / watches **(i)** training videos most of the time. Tom's colleague Martin writes / write / written **(j)** reports. Tom often do / did / does **(k)** some sports or helped / helps / help **(l)** other firemen: They cleaned / clean / cleans **(m)** the fire engines and the equipment or teach / taught / teaches **(n)** new firefighters. Tom says / said / say **(o)**: "I likes / like / liked **(p)** to be a fireman!" Sometimes the fire station has / have / had **(q)** a visit from pupils or other groups. Then Tom try / tried / tries **(r)** to explain everything and what a great job it am / is / are **(s)** to be a firefighter.

Zwischen zwei Zischlauten wird der Vokal **e** (ausgesprochen **[ɪ]**) eingeschoben, um die Aussprache zu erleichtern.

freeze → freez**e**s catch → catch**e**s kiss → kiss**e**s wish → wish**e**s

123 ★

Bilden Sie die ***ing*-Form** zu folgenden Verben.

a) do ________	**b)** run ________	**c)** smile ________
d) lie ________	**e)** travel ________	**f)** sit ________
g) argue ________	**h)** swim ________	**i)** work ________
j) leave ________	**k)** be ________	**l)** have ________

124

★

Bilden Sie die verneinten Formen der folgenden Verben im **present simple**. Verwenden Sie Kurzformen, wenn möglich.

a) is *isn't*
b) do ____
c) have ____
d) can ____
e) does ____
f) are ____
g) work ____
h) stands ____
i) need ____
j) am ____
k) goes ____
l) has ____

125

★

Sie beobachten das Treiben auf einem Wochenmarkt. Was passiert gerade? Schreiben Sie die Verben im **present progressive** in die Lücken.

A small girl ____ (buy) **(a)** carrots from a market stall. At another stall a lot of people ____ (stand) **(b)** in a queue to buy fresh fish. A father and his two children ____ (look) **(c)** at fruit. In the next row a woman ____ (sell) **(d)** flowers. You ____ (check) **(e)** your shopping list. "I ____ (carry) **(f)** a lot of shopping bags already!", you ____ (think) **(g)**. The next moment you ____ (stumble) **(h)** over a cat with a piece of fish in its mouth. The cat ____ (run) **(i)** away as quick as lightning.

Die **progressive**-Form + **always** kann Ärger über eine (schlechte) Gewohnheit anzeigen, z. B.:

Maggie, our cat, **is always bringing** mice home for dinner. She can't see why we don't want to eat them ...
Ständig bringt unsere Katze Maggie Mäuse zum Abendessen mit. Sie sieht einfach nicht ein, warum wir sie nicht essen wollen ...

126 ★★

Welche Begriffe aus der Box sind Signalwörter für das **present simple** und welche zeigen das **present progressive** an? Markieren Sie eine Gruppe.

always · at the moment · every day · just · normally · now · often · right now · sometimes · these days · this summer · this week · never · usually

127 ★★

Welche **Kurzantwort** passt zu welcher Frage? Ordnen Sie zu.

a) Is Mike driving the school bus today?	___ A No, he doesn't.
b) Do the children have sports every Monday?	___ B Yes, they are.
c) Are they having fun right now?	___ C Yes, we are.
d) Does Jenny go to school by bike?	___ D Yes, he has.
e) Have you got a bus ticket?	___ E No, they don't.
f) Hasn't Matt got a new motorbike?	___ F No, I haven't.
g) Does he take you for a ride sometimes?	___ G Yes, he is.
h) Are you having a good time?	___ H Yes, she does.

128 ★★

Wie lautet eine korrekt formulierte Antwort auf folgende Fragen? Entscheiden Sie sich für eine Möglichkeit.

a) Which plane is he taking? – He **take / takes / is taking** the ten o'clock plane.

b) What plans do you have? – I **don't have / haven't / hasn't** any plans so far.

c) Where does she go to school? – She **go / does go / goes** to Markham High.

d) Aren't you staying the night? – No, I **aren't / am not / don't**.

129
★★

Was ist hier richtig: **present simple** oder **progressive**? Bilden Sie je nach Zusammenhang die richtige Form. Achtung: **Present simple** und **progressive** können auch mit Bezug auf zukünftige Ereignisse verwendet werden!

a) Mr Parker always ______________ (take) a coffee from the coffeeshop to his office in the morning. Today he ______________ (not go) to the coffeeshop because he is late.

b) I never ______________ (go) into town by car during the rush hour.

c) We ______________ (have) a lot of barbecues this summer.

d) It ______________ (be) a fact that the moon ______________ (cause) high and low tides.

e) ______________ you ______________ (know) if it is true that lots of people in Switzerland ______________ (speak) several languages fluently?

f) In his book *The Adventures of Huckleberry Finn* Mark Twain ______________ (describe) how the two runaways Huck and Jim ______________ (meet) and ______________ (decide) to go off together. They ______________ (travel) down the river on a raft and ______________ (have) lots of exciting adventures.

g) ______________ our basketball team ______________ (not play) terribly this season?

h) Dad ______________ (mow) the lawn at the moment. My little sister ______________ (help) him. She ______________ (hold) the wire of Dad's electric lawnmower. – Why ______________ she ______________ (do) that? – So that the blades ______________ (not cut) the wire.

i) The buses ______________ (run) every half hour. – I needn't take the bus. I ______________ (come) home with Jenny and Paul, remember?

!

Verben, die einen Zustand ausdrücken, werden normalerweise nicht in der **progressive**-Form verwendet. Bei einigen Verben ist das **progressive** mit veränderter Bedeutung möglich. Sie drücken dann eine vorübergehende Tätigkeit aus.

The house **has** two sleeping rooms. (Zustand)	Sam **is having** a nap. (vorübergehende Tätigkeit)

130 ★★

Kreisen Sie die Verben ein, die normalerweise nicht im **present progressive** verwendet werden.

be · become · believe · belong · cook · drive · eat

feel · get · grow · have · hear · know · like · look

paint · put · read · see · seem · sit · sound

speak · take · think · walk · want · work

131 ★★★

Übersetzen Sie. Achten Sie darauf, wann das **present simple** und wann das **present progressive** angewendet werden muss.

a) *Wir geben heute eine Party. Mel arbeitet gerade in der Küche, während ich die Getränke und Cocktails vorbereite. Aber ich weiß nicht, was Jack gerade tut. Kümmert er sich nicht um das Feuer?*

____

____

____

b) *Terry, ich weiß, dass du keine Spinnen magst, aber du bist kindisch, wenn du diese kleine hier nicht selbst rausbringen willst.*

____

____

c) *Die Johnsons verbringen ihren Urlaub oft in Australien. Sie gehen tauchen oder segeln, und danach entspannen sie sich immer noch eine Woche am Strand.*

d) *In den Alpen benötigen Sie im Winter Schneeketten.*

Je nachdem, was man ausdrücken will, ist die **simple**- oder die **progressive**-Form korrekt:

Tanya **is living** in Cardiff because she has got a fixed-term job there.
Normally she **lives** in Stuttgart.
Tanya lebt zurzeit in Cardiff, weil sie eine befristete Stelle dort hat. Normalerweise lebt sie in Stuttgart.

132 ★★★

Können Sie die Wörter wieder zu Sätzen zusammensetzen? Achten Sie dabei auf die richtige Stellung von Adverbien der Zeit und Häufigkeit.

a) every evening | the dog | Mr Baxter | out | takes | .

b) cycle | you | in summer | always | to work | do | ?

c) normally | I | not | to work | cycle | when | it | is | do | cold and wet | .

d) in the garden | they | are | in the morning | often | .

Past simple und progressive

133 ★

Schreiben Sie alle **past simple**-Formen auf, die sich in der Wortschlange verstecken. Wie lauten deren Infinitive? Schreiben Sie sie dazu.

sellsawrtookwreadthwentshdiddsaidmadehadknewwhatewrotewereubuiltdrover

saw (see), ______________________________

____

____

134 ★

Wie lauten die korrekten **past simple**-Formen? Wählen Sie je eine aus.

a) Dad **speaks / speak / spoke** to Mrs Carstairs yesterday.

b) I **think / thought / thinked** he **stay / stayed / stays** at the office until late.

c) No, he **were / was / been** at home around six.

d) He **say / says / said** he **worked / work / works** late on Monday instead.

e) **Did / Does / Done** Susie **comes / came / come** home yet?

f) No, she **call / called / calls** to say that she **change / changed / chided** shifts.

g) **Did / Do / Done** you **written / write / wrote** your letter to Mom last week?

h) No, I **done / did / does** it only yesterday.

135 ★

Schreiben Sie die richtigen **past simple**-Formen in die Lücke.

a) Yesterday we ____________ (be) bored, so we ____________ (go) out.

b) Last night I ______________________ (not watch) television.

c) ____________ they ____________ (have) their first concert on Saturday?

d) The men ____________ (go) jogging last week.

e) Karen ______ (put) the chairs on the terrace last Saturday.

f) Bill ______ (give) me a call a few days ago.

g) I ______ (meet) him in town yesterday afternoon.

h) It ______ (not be) raining last night when Joe ______ (have) an accident.

i) The kids ______ (not make) their beds yesterday morning.

j) ______ Jamie ______ (cook) you dinner last week?

k) Yes, and we ______ (bring) the wine.

136 ★

Füllen Sie die Lücken mit dem passenden Verb aus dem Kasten. Entscheiden Sie sich dabei jeweils für das richtige Hilfsverb was oder were.

feeling • playing • reading • shining • speaking • swimming • waiting • writing

a) We ______ at the traffic lights when the accident happened.

b) The sun ______, so we went for a walk.

c) I didn't go to work, because I ______ ill.

d) When they came round I ______ a book.

e) Brian broke his leg while he ______ football.

f) She ______ this letter of application half the night.

g) The girls ______ in the pool all afternoon.

h) ______ you ______ to her on the phone all that time?

137 ★★

Ihre Nichte ruft aus dem Zeltlager an, aber die Leitung ist gestört. Sie müssen stets nachfragen, was gerade los war, als etwas Neues passierte.

climb ▪ get into a panic ▪ have a shower ▪ tell us off ▪ try to escape from

a) Mr Marks ... when we all noticed a strange noise.

What was Mr Marks doing when you noticed a strange noise?

– He was telling us off.

b) We were ... Mr Marks when a skunk suddenly appeared.

c) Everybody ... about the skunk when Carol turned up.

d) I ... a tree when the skunk found me.

e) Carol and I ... to get rid of the smell when the power went off.

138 ★★

Sie haben immer noch nicht alles verstanden und müssen Ihre Nichte erneut fragen. Wandeln Sie die Nebensätze mit ***when*** aus Übung 137 in Fragen um.

a) ... when we all noticed a strange noise.

→ *When did you all notice a strange noise?*

b) When Mr Marks began to scream ...

➞ ______________________________

c) ... when Carol turned up.

➞ ______________________________

d) ... when the skunk found me.

➞ ______________________________

e) ... when the power went off.

➞ ______________________________

Auch in Antworten auf Fragen mit **when** verwendet man das **past simple**, z. B.:

When did you first **visit** Canada? – I think it **was** about seven years ago.

139 ★★

Können Sie die Verben im **past simple** wiederherstellen? Sie können aus mehreren Teilen bestehen und manchmal müssen Apostrophe gesetzt werden.

a) __________ you __________ (addhive) a nice holiday?

b) __________ you __________ (liddpay) the guitar at the concert?

c) When I __________ (saw) a child, I __________ (nliditked) reading.

d) __________ they __________ (ddsnied) us an invitation?

e) We __________ (ifninddtd) an invitation in the mail.

f) Luckily it __________ (trainindd) on Lara's birthday.

g) What __________ we __________ (giddet) as a present for her?

h) Why __________ Carol __________ (oddting) for a walk with the dog?

140 ★★

Tragen Sie die korrekte **past simple**-Form der Verben in das Kreuzworträtsel ein. Achten Sie auf unregelmäßige Formen.

a) convince **b)** quit **c)** lay **d)** perceive
e) elaborate **f)** juxtapose **g)** negotiate **h)** strike
i) forbid **j)** oversleep **k)** resell **l)** reply

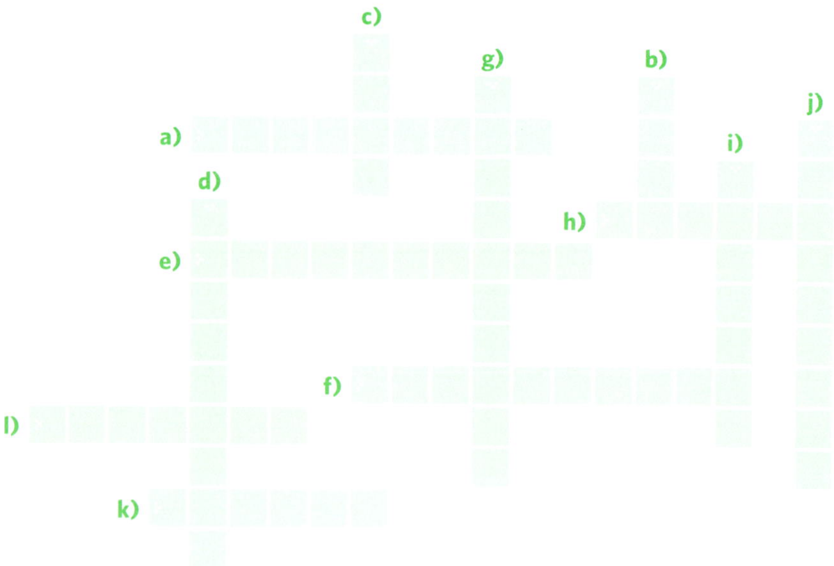

141 ★★★

Was passierte im Garten? Wählen Sie die passenden Verben aus und bilden Sie jeweils die korrekte Zeitform: **past simple** oder **progressive**.

While our dog Sam was sleeping, the neighbour's cat Tilly ________________ **(a)** all his food. Tilly ________________ **(b)** under our car when Sam realized his food was gone. Another cat slowly ________________ **(c)** into our garden while Sam was sniffing to find the thief. When the other cat was walking past his hut, Sam ________________ **(d)** her. While Sam was hunting the intruder, Tilly ________________ **(e)** into Sam's hut, ________________ **(f)** his ball and ________________ **(g)** back to her own garden.

eat
go
hide
notice
run
sneak
take

142 ★★★

Ordnen Sie die Bilder den Sätzen zu und ergänzen Sie die Sätze mit der jeweils richtigen Verbform im **past simple** oder **progressive**.

A

B

C

D

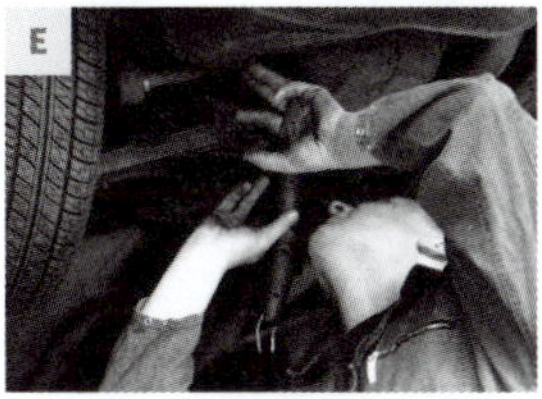
E

F

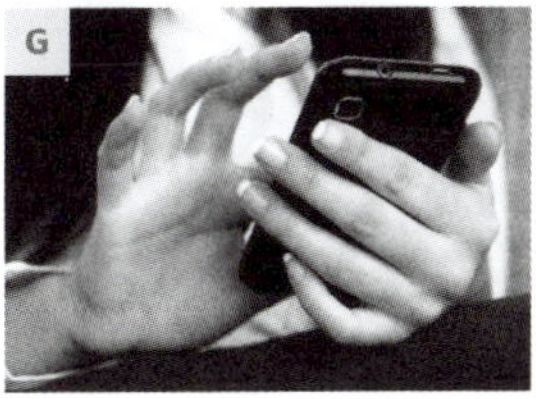
G

H

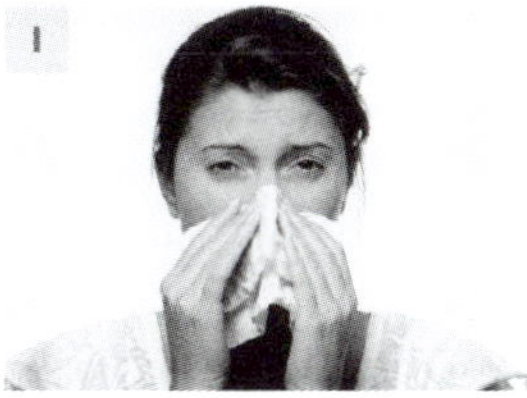
I

_E_ **a)** What were you doing yesterday? – I _repaired_ Joe's van.

____ **b)** Janet ________ at some plans with her boss on the building site when Tina ________ her a message.

____ **c)** Tara ________ barefoot in the sand in October. Then she ________ a cold. While her husband ________ to the office the next morning, she stayed in bed.

____ **d)** Lilo ________ beach volleyball on Sunday. After the game she ________ some water. Then she went home and ________ in her hammock to relax with a book.

143 ★★★

Übersetzen Sie, aber nicht wortwörtlich. Achtung: In den folgenden Sätzen unterscheiden sich das Deutsche und das Englische besonders bei den Verben.

a) *Kam deine Präsentation gut an? – Ja.*

b) *Was hast du danach gemacht? – Ich bin etwas trinken gegangen.*

c) *Wohin bist du gegangen? – In die neue Bar in der Innenstadt.*

d) *Wie hat es dir gefallen? – Ich fand es großartig.*

144 ★★★

Wie geht es richtig nach dem ersten Wort weiter? Setzen Sie Kommas, wenn nötig. Manchmal gibt es mehrere Möglichkeiten.

a) Carol's Mom | wasn't | about | so soon | happy | marrying | them | .

b) When | this house | were | they | that | they | sure | wanted | to buy | ?

c) Josh | when | they | at university | the estate agent | got | acquainted with | were | still | both | .

d) While | Josh | the painting | Carol | was doing | was laying | the carpets | .

____

____

e) The removal van | while | to the kitchen | putting | they | arrived | were | the finishing touches | .

____

____

f) When | left | Carol | and | Josh | a glass of champagne | the removal men | were drinking | .

____

____

Present perfect simple und progressive

145 ★

Wie lauten die **past participles** zu den folgenden Verbformen?

a) have *had*

b) make ____________

c) answer ____________

d) get ____________

e) read ____________

f) think ____________

g) was ____________

h) did ____________

i) paid ____________

j) watched ____________

k) found ____________

l) looked ____________

!

Im Deutschen bildet man das **Perfekt** mit „haben“ oder mit „sein“. Im Englischen werden die **perfect-**Formen stets mit einer Form von **have** gebildet.

She **has** (= She’s) already gone home. *Sie ist schon nach Hause gegangen.*

146 ★

Schreiben Sie die Verben in die jeweils verneinte Form um. Verwenden Sie dabei Kurzformen, wenn möglich.

a) she's flown *she hasn't flown / she's not flown*

b) he's been flying ______

c) they've worked ______

d) you've been managing ______

e) I've done ______

f) we've started ______

147 ★★

Welche Fragen und Antworten gehören zueinander? Achtung Glatteis: Hier werden auch andere Zeiten als das **present perfect simple** verwendet.

a) Did she make a good impression yesterday? ___ A No, it hasn't.

b) Haven't you finished your homework yet? ___ B Yes, it is.

c) Hasn't it been discussed enough? ___ C No, we haven't.

d) Is it made by hand? ___ D Yes, they had.

e) Hadn't they seen the accident? ___ E Yes, she did.

f) Have we agreed on that matter? ___ F No, I haven't.

148 ★★

Ergänzen Sie die folgenden Sätze jeweils mit der richtigen Form des **present perfect simple** und der passenden Präposition (**for** oder **since**).

a) We *have felt* (feel) ill *for* three weeks.

b) I ______ (not take) any medicine ______ last weekend.

c) Paul ______ (have) a soar throat ______ Wednesday.

d) Richard ______ (not eat) anything ______ four days.

e) ______ (you, drink) any alcohol ______ Christmas?

f) My parents really ______ (enjoy) the time ______ my father went into retirement.

g) They ______ (go) on a journey to Brazil ______ six weeks, for example.

!

Zeitangaben werden im **present perfect** mit **for** oder **since** gemacht.
For beschreibt einen Zeitraum, **since** nennt einen Zeitpunkt.

I haven't seen Lucy **for two years/since 1998**.
Ich habe Lucy seit zwei Jahren/seit 1998 nicht gesehen.

149 ★★★

Bilden Sie Sätze im **present perfect simple**. Achten Sie darauf, ob es sich um eine Aussage, eine Frage oder eine Verneinung handelt.

a) I | just | see | your sister | hairdresser's | .

______

b) not | they | finish | doing | her hair | yet | ?

______

c) she | never | look | better | her life | .

______

d) you | have | look at | flowers | yet | ?

______

e) you | ever | meet | bridegroom | ?

______

150 ★★★

Ergänzen Sie die jeweils richtige Verbform: **present perfect simple** oder **progressive**.

a) Some construction workers ______________________ (repair) potholes in our street since the early morning. The noise is deafening.

b) Oh no! ______________________ (you, really, wait) for me for three hours?

c) I'm sorry, but I ______________________ (not see) Tina.

______________________ (you, try) to reach her on her mobile?

d) ______________________ (Jerry, not be) a member of the chess club for over thirty years now? But he still loses a game sometimes.

e) We ______________________ (feel) so at home in Florida since we came here

in November! We ______________________ (enjoy) every single minute.

f) Stop working now! You ______________________ (sit) at that laptop for ages.

Present perfect oder past simple?

151 ★

Hier verstecken sich **past simple**-Formen und **past participles**. Schreiben Sie jeweils Lösung und Form auf (ps = past simple, pp = past participle).

a) knospe ______________

b) abeng ______________

c) ense ______________

d) kroeb ______________

e) nego ______________

f) edrvo ______________

g) tea ______________

h) wonnk ______________

i) ketan ______________

j) gofort ______________

152 ★

Finden Sie die Signalwörter für das **present perfect simple** bzw. für das **past simple** heraus? Markieren Sie eine der beiden Gruppen.

ago already ever for
in 2001 just last week last year never
since so far this year three years ago
until up to now yesterday yet

153 ★★

Vervollständigen Sie diese Sätze, indem Sie die richtige Form des Verbs und die passende Zeit auswählen: **past simple** oder **present perfect**.

a) Joel has run away / ran away / run away from his wedding last Saturday.

b) Jenny has flew / has flown / flew to Berlin three times this year.

c) A young girl has swum / swam / has swim across the English Channel some time ago.

d) The police found / has found / have found the driver who has overtaken / overtook / has overtook the school bus at the stop yesterday and took / have taken / has taken away his driving licence already.

154 ★★

Welche Zeitform muss jeweils verwendet werden: **past simple** oder **present perfect**?

a) I ______________ (feel) ill last week.

b) They ______________ (have) a fever since Tuesday.

c) ______________ (you, be) ill this week?

d) We ______________ (not go) to work yesterday.

e) I ______________ (cut) my finger – it hurts!

f) She ______________ (take) the tablets last night.

155 ★★

Diese Sätze sind durcheinandergeraten. Verbinden Sie die passenden Fragen und Antworten.

a) Has he been to church this morning?	___ A He might have.
b) Wasn't she waiting there?	___ B No, I haven't.
c) Did she ask herself what happened?	___ C Yes, they did.
d) Has he left for good?	___ D He must have been.
e) Have you ever thought this might happen?	___ E Yes, she was.
f) Did somebody cancel all the festivities?	___ F Of course she did.

156 ★★★

Welche Zeitform ist hier im Englischen die richtige? Übersetzen Sie.

a) *Als Maya klein war, wollte sie Feuerwehrfrau werden.*

____

b) *Warst du je auf Jamaica?*

____

c) *Habt ihr den Krimi gesehen, als er im Fernsehen kam?*

____

d) *Sue hat ein neues Haus gekauft, aber ihr altes hat sie noch nicht verkauft.*

____

Auch ohne Zeitangaben kann man meist erkennen, ob die Handlung einen Bezug zur Gegenwart hat oder nicht, z. B.:

Sting **has written** the song 'Roxanne'.	*Sting hat das Lied ‚Roxanne' geschrieben.*
Mark Twain **wrote** many novels.	*Mark Twain hat viele Romane geschrieben.*

Past perfect simple und progressive

157 ★

Tragen Sie für die angegebenen Verben die fehlenden Buchstaben der **present** und **past participles** ein.

		present participles	past participles
a)	be	b ___ ___ ng	b ___ ___ n
b)	have	h ___ ___ ___ ng	ha ___
c)	do	d ___ ___ ___ g	do ___ ___
d)	teach	t ___ ___ ch ___ ng	t ___ ___ ght
e)	learn	l ___ ___ rn ___ ___ g	l ___ ___ rnt
f)	tell	t ___ l ___ ___ ng	t ___ l ___
g)	buy	b ___ ___ ___ ng	b ___ ___ ght
h)	keep	ke ___ p ___ ___ g	k ___ ___ t
i)	swim	s ___ ___ m ___ ___ ___ g	s ___ ___ m

158 ★

Beantworten Sie die Fragen und verwenden Sie dafür **Kurzantworten**.

a) Had they gone to Spain already? Yes, ______________________.

b) Had she been working all day? No, ______________________.

c) Hadn't Mike told you everything? No, ______________________.

d) Had you already planned to move there? Yes, ______________________.

e) Hadn't I hung out the washing before we went? Yes, ______________________.

f) Had we met before that evening? No, ______________________.

g) Hadn't Todd and Joe been fishing then? No, ______________________.

159 ★

Um welche Vergangenheitsform handelt es sich? Kreuzen Sie an.

	past perfect simple	past perfect progressive
a) Max had been visiting us.	☐	☐
b) Had they gone home?	☐	☐
c) I had been waiting.	☐	☐
d) Tony had been really tired.	☐	☐
e) Had she had her hair cut?	☐	☐
f) It hadn't been a nice afternoon.	☐	☐
g) Had Thomas been working all day?	☐	☐

160 ★★

Schreiben Sie die **simple**-Formen ins **past perfect simple** und die **progressive**-Formen ins **past perfect progressive** um.

a) were having ______________________

b) wasn't reading ______________________

c) has been raining ______________________

d) has been late ______________________

e) cycled ______________________

f) didn't swim ______________________

Das **past perfect** wird mit einer Form von **had** (+ past participle) gebildet.

He **had** worked. *Er hatte gearbeitet.* She **had** gone. *Sie war gegangen.*

Die **progressive**-Formen werden mit einer Form von **be** (+ present participle) gebildet:

He had **been** working. She had **been** going.

161 ★★

Hier verstecken sich Verben im **past perfect simple** oder **progressive** in bis zu vier Einzelteilen (auch Verneinungen). Ergänzen Sie ggf. Apostrophe.

a) Where ______________ he ______________ (neadheb) for all those years?

b) Had the dogs ______________ (gunbenreinn) all the way before we met?

c) They ______________________________ (dauntbaenngheirg) for a long time before they made a fresh start.

d) She ______________________ (daadbeingenreh) since her parents went out.

e) I ______________ (nadhohugttht) about visitors before the doorbell rang.

Das **past perfect simple** wird für <u>abgeschlossene Handlungen</u> verwendet, die in der Vergangenheit <u>vor</u> einer anderen, vergangenen Handlung stattfanden (oft mit **after**, **before**).

Das **past perfect progressive** wird für <u>länger andauernde Handlungen</u> verwendet, die <u>vor</u> einer anderen, vergangenen Handlung stattfanden (oft mit **all day/ night/...**, **when**, **since**, **for**).

162 ★★★

Setzen Sie die Vorgaben im **past perfect simple** oder **progressive** ein.

a) Todd ______________________________ *(hatte gewartet)* at the station for two hours when Linda arrived finally.

b) Mrs Miff told me that the dog which ______________________________ *(hatte gebissen)* her belonged to Mr Parker.

c) Sally knew how to knit because she ______________________________ *(hatte gelernt)* it at school.

d) Lance realized that the car which ______________________________ *(war gefolgt)* him all day was his ex-girlfriend's.

163 ★★★

Welches Foto passt zu welchem Satz? Wie lauten dann die zeitlich korrekten Verbformen: **past perfect simple** oder **progressive**?

A

B

C

D

E

F

___ **a)** After that bear ______________________ at us in a quite unfriendly way we left our picnic basket to him without any argument.

___ **b)** The doctor ______________________ reports all morning before she came to speak with me.

___ **c)** The play had been extremely boring until the two suddenly ______________________ with each other.

___ **d)** Before the alarm started to ring at the library everybody ______________________ quietly.

___ **e)** She told me that she ______________________ about her next holiday when we met.

___ **f)** When he came to work he ______________________ the paper already.

!

Die Kurzformen von **had** und **would** sind identisch:

I'd = **I had** oder **I would**

Past perfect und past simple

164 ★

Kreuzen Sie an, zu welchen Zeiten die Formen gehören.

	past simple	past perfect simple/ progressive
a) hadn't had	☐	☐
b) had	☐	☐
c) didn't go	☐	☐
d) had been doing	☐	☐
e) were done	☐	☐
f) had been	☐	☐
g) was asleep	☐	☐
h) had read	☐	☐

Das **past perfect** mit **had** wird manchmal mit „haben" und manchmal mit „sein" übersetzt, z. B.:

I **had** taken a shower.	*Ich hatte geduscht.*
I **had** fallen asleep.	*Ich war eingeschlafen.*

165 ★

Zu den Fragen gibt es je ein passendes **question tag**. Kreuzen Sie es an.

a) She did fly to Australia finally,
- ☐ A did she?
- ☐ B didn't she?
- ☐ C wasn't she?

b) They hadn't had too much bread,
- ☐ A didn't they?
- ☐ B hadn't they?
- ☐ C had they?

c) It had been a nice evening,
- ☐ A was it?
- ☐ B had it?
- ☐ C hadn't it?

d) You tried to help her,
- ☐ A weren't you?
- ☐ B didn't you?
- ☐ C hadn't you?

166 ★★

Wie lauten die **Infinitive** zu folgenden Formen? Die angegebenen Buchstaben der Lösungswörter ergeben ein weiteres **past participle**.

a) trodden ______ (5. Buchstabe)

b) spread ______ (4. Buchstabe)

c) blew ______ (2. Buchstabe)

d) rose ______ (2. Buchstabe)

e) forgave ______ (6. Buchstabe)

f) frozen ______ (4. und 2. Buchstabe)

g) bent ______ (2. und 4. Buchstabe)

Lösung: ______

167 ★★

Überlegen Sie, welche Handlung(en) jeweils zuerst geschah(en) und setzen Sie **past simple** oder **past perfect simple** ein.

a) After Josh *had missed* (miss) the plane he *had to wait* (have to wait) four hours for another flight.

b) Maya ______ (tell) me about the books she ______ (read) in her previous semester.

c) Nicki ______ (leave) already when Mia ______ (see) that she ______ (forget) her teddy.

d) Before Annie ______ (start) to work in the hospital she ______ (bring) the children to the kindergarten already.

e) By the time the fire brigade ______ (arrive) the neighbours ______ (manage) to bring the fire under control.

Im **past perfect** stehen Handlungen, die zeitlich vor Handlungen im **past simple** ablaufen. Mit der Verwendung des **past perfect** betont man, dass diese Handlungen zeitlich nacheinander erfolgen.

You **had been working/had worked** for ages before I **found** you.
Du hattest seit Ewigkeiten gearbeitet, bevor ich dich fand.

168 ★★

Welche Satzteile gehören zusammen? Manchmal gibt es mehrere Möglichkeiten.

a) Leo had been dating Pia since June ___ A she finally went to the doctor.

b) Josh and Mike were watching TV ___ B until those cats made a din.

c) A mole was digging up my garden ___ C before he asked her to marry him.

d) The kids were sleeping ___ D while I was enjoying my holiday.

e) After Rina had been coughing for ages ___ E when a power cut made the screen go blank.

169 ★★★

Lisa schreibt eine E-Mail an eine Freundin in den USA. Füllen Sie die Lücken mit den jeweils passenden **Zeitformen der Vergangenheit**.

From: ______ To: ______

Hi Tamara!

It ______ (be) **(a)** a while since you last ______ (send) **(b)** me an e-mail. How ______ your job interviews ______ (go) **(c)**? ______ (you, get) **(d)** a new job yet? When we ______ (talk) **(e)** last month, you ______ (tell) **(f)** me about your two favourite jobs. You ______ (say) **(g)** you ______ (look) **(h)** at hundreds of ads before you ______ (find) **(i)** these. Now I want to know: ______ you ______ (manage) **(j)** to get one of them?

Best, Lisa

170 ★★★

Die Sätze sind durcheinandergeraten. Können Sie sie – jeweils mit den richtigen **Zeitformen der Vergangenheit** – wieder zusammensetzen?

a) since | watch TV | six o'clock | Nick | .

____

b) Andy | before | we | call to tell | about his baby | eat | us | .

____

c) Tia | the doorbell | a bubble bath | when | have | ring | yesterday evening | .

____

171 ★★★

Übersetzen Sie und achten Sie dabei auf die korrekte Wiedergabe der Zeiten und der Abfolge der Ereignisse.

a) *Ich war letzte Woche nicht arbeiten, weil ich am Sonntag krank geworden war.*

____

____

b) *Mia hatte schon immer in Lübeck gelebt, bis sie letztes Jahr nach Oslo umziehen musste.*

____

____

____

c) *Wir wollten Thomas besuchen, aber er hatte mal wieder zu viel zu tun.*

____

____

Future tenses

172 ★

Bilden Sie mit den Vorgaben das **going to-future**. Verwenden Sie Kurzformen, wenn möglich.

a) I (have) *I'm going to have*

b) she (not make) ______

c) they (do) ______

d) Mike (travel) ______

e) you (not stay up) ______

f) Mr and Mrs Knox (go out) ______

173 ★

Wie lauten diese Sätze im **will-future** jeweils verneint bzw. bejaht?

a) Lina will be here after dinner. ______

b) She'll help you with the cooking. ______

c) ______ I'm sure the rain won't stop soon.

d) We'll watch a movie tonight. ______

e) ______ The Smiths won't visit Cádiz.

174 ★

Hier verstecken sich Signalwörter für die **future tenses**.

untilfirsttimetomorroworsttnextyearearringinten
daysyetthedayaftertomorrowwheneverforevermore
intwoyearssincewhennextmonth

______

______

175 ★★

Schreiben Sie die Vorgaben jeweils in die **progressive-** oder **simple-**Form des **will-future** bzw. **future perfect** um.

	simple form	progressive form
a)	Sam will go	*Sam will be going*
b)	they won't hear	________
c)	she'll have talked	________
d)	________	I won't have been driving
e)	________	you'll be coming back
f)	________	it won't be selling
g)	we'll have done	________

176 ★★

Welche Antwort ist die Richtige? Lesen Sie die Fragen im **will-future**, **present simple** und **going to-future** und entscheiden Sie.

a) Where are you going to stay?

- ☐ A I'll stay at the Hilton.
- ☐ B I'm going to stay with friends.
- ☐ C I stay at home.

b) Will the weather be nice in Rome?

- ☐ A Yes, it'll be nice.
- ☐ B No, it's going to rain.
- ☐ C Yes, it's fine.

c) When does your train leave?

- ☐ A It'll leave at 15:35.
- ☐ B It leaves at 15:35.
- ☐ C It's going to leave at 15:35.

d) Won't she be at Josie's?

- ☐ A No, she's not going to be there.
- ☐ B No, she's not at Josie's.
- ☐ C No, she'll probably be at the gym.

!

Im Englischen kann etwas Zukünftiges auch mit dem **simple present** ausgedrückt werden. Grob gesagt gilt das für feststehende Ereignisse wie Feste, Fahrpläne oder Veranstaltungen.

This year Christmas Eve **is** on a Monday.

177 ★★

Bilden Sie Sätze aus den durcheinander geratenen Wörtern und verwenden Sie **Kurzformen**, wenn möglich. Achten Sie auf Fragen und Verneinungen.

a) have | if | to take | it | rains | we | the car | will | .

____

b) going | Jim | with | you | to help | is | your tax return | ?

____

c) the Macks | going | not | this year | are | their holidays | in Italy | to spend | .

____

d) tired | not | after work | Sally | be | will | ?

____

e) will | I | be | to Cuba | with Caty | flying | tomorrow | .

____

178 ★★

Vervollständigen Sie die E-Mail an eine Freundin in Wales.

'll be picking me up • is going to handle • 'll be able to • 'll like • 'm taking • arrives • 'm going to live

From: ____________ To: ____________

Hello Julia!

Guess what? I ____________ **(a)** in Wales for a while! We ____________ **(b)** meet every weekend if we want to. I ____________ **(c)** the ferry next Saturday. A removal firm ____________ **(d)** the larger things. I just hope I ____________ **(e)** the rooms I have managed to rent in advance – and the landlady ... The ferry ____________ **(f)** in Newport at 16.25 on Saturday. I expect you ____________!
See you soon, Jill

179 ★★

Überlegen Sie, ob die Sätze mit dem **will-future**, **going to-future** oder **present progressive** vervollständigt werden müssen.

a) Look at Toby! He ______________ (be) sick any moment.

b) You ______________ (have) an accident if you drive on these icy roads.

c) I'm sure that in a hundred years people ______________ (live) on Mars.

d) Tom has just called. He ______________ (come) round tonight.

e) Jill ______________ (leave) for Wales soon. She has already booked the ferry.

f) The fridge is out of order. – What ______________ (we, do) about it?

present simple: für Fahrpläne, Veranstaltungen, Feiertage
present progressive: fest vereinbarte Handlung oder Vorhaben in der Zukunft
going to-future: Ideen, Pläne, Vorhersagen anhand von deutlichen Anzeichen
will-future: spontane Entscheidung, Vermutung, Vorhersage (z. B. über Wetter)
future progressive: zu erwartende Ereignisse, andauernde Handlung in der Zukunft

180 ★★★

Ordnen Sie den Beispielsätzen jeweils die Sprechabsicht dahinter zu.

a) I'll leave at one o'clock.
b) I'll be leaving at one o'clock.
c) I'm going to leave at one o'clock.
d) I'll have left at one o'clock.
e) I'm leaving at one o'clock.
f) I leave at one o'clock.

___ A Plan, Idee
___ B festes Vorhaben
___ C Vermutung oder Vorhersage
___ D Ankunft/Abreise laut Fahrplan
___ E in der Zukunft abgeschlossenes Ereignis
___ F Ereignis, das sich ohne Zutun ergeben wird

181

★★★

Welches Foto und welches Verb passt jeweils zu welchem Satz? Ordnen Sie sie zu und bilden Sie dann die passende **Zukunftsform**.

a) have time to relax

b) dance the tango

c) have to get up

d) take place

e) have breakfast

f) leave

___ A Tomorrow morning we ______________________ at 7 o'clock.

___ B Our plane to Rio ______________________ at 12.35 a.m.

___ C The next morning we ______________________ in the hotel room.

___ D I'm sure we ______________________ on the beach before the wedding.

___ E The champagne reception ______________________ in the afternoon.

___ F By the end of the party we ______________________ at least a dozen times.

!

Im Deutschen wird auch oft das Präsens für zukünftige Ereignisse bzw. Handlungen verwendet. Aber Achtung beim Übersetzen: Im Englischen ist für die Wahl der Zeitform <u>nur die Sprechabsicht</u> (Vorhersage, Vermutung, Verabredung, ...) wichtig!

182 ★★★

Übersetzen Sie. Überlegen Sie, welche **Zeitform der Zukunft** jeweils benötigt wird.

a) *Heute Nachmittag gehe ich zum Arzt - ich habe einen Termin um 15 Uhr.*

____

____

b) *Ich weiß nicht genau, wo ich den nächsten Sommer verbringen werde, aber ich würde sehr gerne nach Frankreich gehen.*

____

____

c) *Wenn du um 18 Uhr vorbeikommst, bin ich bis dahin fertig mit Gärtnern.*

____

____

d) *Ich bin sicher, du wirst deinen Urlaub in der Türkei nächsten Monat genießen.*

____

____

183 ★★★

Wählen Sie die richtige Zeitform: **will-future progressive**, **future perfect** oder **future perfect progressive**.

a) We can't meet on Friday because I __________________ (visit) my parents.

b) Tony __________________ (mow) the lawn by eight o'clock, he says.

c) Don't call me at seven because we __________________ (have) dinner then.

d) By next summer I __________________ (save) enough money to visit you in Australia.

e) By the time Jane finishes her exams she __________________ (study) for three years.

Conditional und conditional perfect

184 ★

Welches **question tag** passt jeweils zu den Sätzen? Unterstreichen Sie.

a) She would do everything for you, **doesn't she / wouldn't she / didn't she**?

b) They shouldn't have missed that, **haven't they / should they / have they**?

c) He would have called us, **wouldn't he / would he / won't he**?

d) You know I would help you if I could, **could I / couldn't I / wouldn't I**?

e) You wouldn't have thought that, **have you / would you / wouldn't you**?

f) We wouldn't tell anybody, **wouldn't we / hadn't we / would we**?

g) It wouldn't have made a difference, **would it / have it / has it**?

185 ★★

Achtung Glatteis: Um welche Zeiten handelt es sich hier: **conditional**, **conditional perfect** oder **past perfect**? Kreuzen Sie an.

	conditional	conditional perfect	past perfect
a) I'd buy	☐	☐	☐
b) he'd bought	☐	☐	☐
c) she'd have bought	☐	☐	☐
d) they'd sold	☐	☐	☐
e) we'd sell	☐	☐	☐
f) you'd have sold	☐	☐	☐
g) it'd been cold	☐	☐	☐
h) it'd be cold	☐	☐	☐
i) it'd have been cold	☐	☐	☐

186 ★★

Ersetzen Sie die Vorgaben durch deren **Kurzformen** (soweit möglich).

a) ________________ (I would rather) go home now.

b) ________________ (would you not enjoy) a wellness weekend?

c) Oh thanks, that ________________ (would not have been) necessary.

d) ________________ (I would like) to have a cup of coffee, please.

e) ________________ (She would never have come back) if she didn't love you.

f) What ________________ (would you do) if it was your car? Sell it or keep it?

187 ★★

Welche Verbform passt in welche Lücke? Wählen Sie aus.

could • could have • should • would be • would do • would like

From: ________ To: ________

Hi Maya,

Do you remember I told you I was preparing some letters of application in English? I was wondering if you ________________ **(a)** me a favour. If I e-mailed you my applications, ________________ **(b)** you perhaps find the time to go over them? I ________________ **(c)** to know if I have to correct anything. If you looked at my papers before I send them off I ________________ **(d)** so relieved. I ________________ **(e)** asked my teacher if she wasn't away on holiday.

Please say you will do it! You know that if you ________________ **(f)** ever need help, you just have to tell me.

With a big THANK YOU for considering it ☺!
Best, Nina

188 ★★★

Setzen Sie die Verben ins **conditional** und bringen Sie dann die Satzteile in die richtige Reihenfolge.

a) the window | close | please | you | ?

____

b) not tell | in your position | I | anybody | .

____

c) to London | she | to Rio | rather | go | or | ?

____

ABC

Häufige Wendungen im **conditional** sind:

I'd like to + infinitive:	I'**d like to go** home.	*Ich möchte gerne nach Hause gehen.*
I'd rather + infinitive:	I'**d rather stay**.	*Ich würde lieber bleiben.*

189 ★★★

Conditional oder **conditional perfect**? Übersetzen Sie die Vorgaben.

a) I ______________ *(würde nicht gehen)* to Italy now. It's too busy.

b) I ______________ *(hätte nicht zugestimmt)* without having known all the details.

c) Luckily you thought to phone. Otherwise we ______________ ______________ *(würden immer noch warten)*.

d) We ______________ *(hätten bemerkt)* a man like that.

Will man das **conditional** ins Deutsche übertragen, verwendet man den Konjunktiv. Das **conditional perfect** wird mit dem Konjunktiv II übersetzt.

Mike **would be** angry.	*Mike wäre wütend.* (ugs.: *Mike würde wütend sein.)*
Mike **would have been** angry.	*Mike wäre wütend gewesen.*

190 ★

Wie lauten diese Aussagesätze in der richtigen **Satzstellung**? Manchmal gibt es mehrere Möglichkeiten.

a) dad | the lawn | mows

____

b) like | her | I

____

c) can | you | Tom | help

____

d) am | I | reading

____

e) invited | the Marksons | us | have

____

f) is | she | her maths homework | doing

____

g) to buy | wants | Tilly | a new car

____

!

Die Grundregel für die korrekte Satzstellung von Aussagesätzen im Englischen lautet:

<u>Subjekt (S)</u>	<u>Prädikat (P)</u>	<u>Objekt (O)</u> (wenn vorhanden)
Mary	is playing	(a game).
I	like	Mary/her.

Achtung: Im Deutschen kann das Objekt auch <u>vor</u> dem Prädikat stehen!

191 ★

Ergänzen Sie die fehlenden **Kommas**.

a) Jenny can you help me please?

b) Do you like chocolate cookies? – Yes I do.

c) Do you like chips as well?

d) Please tell me the truth.

e) Well isn't the weather nice today?

f) Have you heard about Lisa's accident? – No I haven't.

192 ★★

Wie werden die **phrasal verbs** richtig in den Satz eingebaut? Kreuzen Sie die korrekten Teilsätze an. Es gibt manchmal mehrere Möglichkeiten.

a) Would you ...

- ☐ A turn on the TV, please?
- ☐ B turn on it, please?
- ☐ C turn the TV on, please?

b) Please ...

- ☐ A go on with your lecture.
- ☐ B go on your lecture with.
- ☐ C go on with it.

c) I'm ...

- ☐ A looking my mobile for.
- ☐ B looking for my mobile.
- ☐ C looking it for.

d) Can you ...

- ☐ A tell Cara and Mia apart?
- ☐ B tell them apart?
- ☐ C tell apart them?

193 ★★

Nach diesen Verben stehen **zwei Objekte**. Können Sie an der Stellung im Satz erkennen, welches davon jeweils betont ist? Unterstreichen Sie es.

a) Tom will show **his friends the car**.

b) Carla didn't say **a single word to me about the whole affair**.

c) Mr Parker described **the new training course to us**.

d) Barry tells **his golden retriever everything**.

194 ★★★

Überprüfen Sie die Sätze. Wo fehlen **Kommas**? Sind die vorhandenen Kommas richtig gesetzt?

a) Jamie who lives downtown is meeting us in front of the cinema.

b) Dad thought those shoes were too expensive, anyway.

c) Mum was angry yesterday because our dog had slept in Timmy's bed.

d) Timmy however didn't see why he should sleep alone.

e) Well it sounds like a good plan, but haven't you forgotten a small point?

f) On the contrary, I think that we have considered everything.

g) Anyway, I would like to go out for dinner, although it's quite late.

h) Look, there's the restaurant that Marc talked about yesterday.

Nicht notwendige Relativsätze werden mit Kommas vom Hauptsatz abgetrennt:

Timmy's dog**, which is a dachshund,** slept in Timmy's bed.

Notwendige Relativsätze stehen ohne Komma:

That's the dog **which slept in Timmy's bed**.

195 ★★★

Formulieren Sie die Sätze so, dass die markierten Wörter betont werden. Stellen Sie die Objekte um oder verwenden Sie **it is/was ... that.**

a) Rob won the **school tennis tournament** last year.

____

b) I can send **you** the CD.

____

c) **Our neighbours** called the fire brigade when they noticed the smoke.

____

196 ★★★

Übersetzen Sie die Sätze ins Englische und achten Sie dabei auf Besonderheiten bei der Satzstellung.

a) *Sie hatte kaum die Tür geöffnet, als die Katze hereinkam.*

____

b) *Herr Harris stellte uns die drei neuen Mathe- und Physiklehrer vor.*

____

c) *Er vergaß nicht nur diesen Termin, sondern auch viele andere.*

____

d) *Das Auto hatte weder einen Platten noch irgendeinen anderen Defekt.*

____

197 ★★★

Können Sie die Sätze wieder richtig zusammensetzen?

a) Lucy | at kindergarten | yesterday afternoon | fell asleep | .

____

b) Mike | too fast | usually | drives | in winter | .

____

c) The gospel choir | last Saturday | sang | at the street party | beautifully | .

____

Eine weitere Grundregel für die Satzstellung im Englischen lautet: **manner – place – time**, d. h. Angaben zu Art und Weise erscheinen <u>vor</u> Angaben zu Ort und Zeit.

	manner	place	time
Lisa looks through her e-mails	**quickly**	**at her desk**	**every morning**.

Lisa geht ihre E-Mails morgens schnell an ihrem Schreibtisch durch.

198 ★

In der Wortschlange verstecken sich 13 **Konjunktionen**. Finden Sie sie?

frommoreafterrimwheresinceneverbeforeendandifforbutontobecausesothisthatwhentowardswhilelongalthough

199 ★

Welche eine bzw. zwei **Konjunktionen** verbinden die Satzteile korrekt?

a) I always take my umbrella with me **because / so that / or** it doesn't rain.

b) Lara didn't want to go out **although / because / and** she felt unwell.

c) **When / If / Where** the music is good we will stay at that club for a while.

d) He didn't look at me **while / after / whereas** he had told me.

e) I didn't know what to do, **yet / therefore / so** I did nothing.

f) The postman rang **when / while / since** I was vacuuming, **otherwise / unless / so** I didn't hear him.

Achten Sie beim Gebrauch von **if** (= *wenn*, *falls*: nicht sicher; Bedingung) und **when** (= *wenn*, *als*: auf jeden Fall; zeitlicher Aspekt) auf den Bedeutungsunterschied, z. B.:

If/When I **go** to Rio, I'**ll watch** the carnival. *Wenn ich nach Rio fahre ...*

Die Konjunktion **while** (= *während*) leitet einen Nebensatz mit bereits laufender Handlung im **past** oder **present progressive** ein, z. B.:

While Brian **was playing** football, he **broke** his leg.

When (**past simple:** = *als*; **present simple:** = *sobald*) leitet einen Nebensatz mit neu einsetzender Handlung im **past** oder **present simple**) ein, z. B.:

We **were waiting** at the traffic lights **when** the crash **happened**.

200 ★★

Ergänzen Sie in den folgenden Sätzen jeweils den in Klammern angegebenen Begriff an der richtigen Stelle.

a) I watch TV and listen to the radio. (both)

____

b) I like reading editorials or the business section. (either)

____

c) Today Bill has read the newspaper and watched a film. (both)

____

d) You can have the fish with boiled potatoes or noodles. (either)

____

e) He likes swimming nor jogging. (neither)

____

201 ★★★

Wählen Sie die richtige **Konjunktion** für die jeweilige Lücke aus.

as if ▪ as soon as ▪ even if ▪ furthermore ▪ however ▪ nevertheless ▪ otherwise ▪ though ▪ unless

__________ **(a)** the children had left, Liz took a deep breath. __________ **(b)** she loved them more than anything, she enjoyed the quietness that didn't occur __________ **(c)** the house was empty. __________ **(d)**, she could do things without interruption. __________ **(e)**, she had to keep an eye on the time, __________ **(f)** she would be surprised by the kids' return. __________ **(g)**, she often forgot the time, __________ **(h)** she tried not to. Then she sometimes felt __________ **(i)** somebody had pressed fast-forward.

202 ★

Schreiben Sie die Wörter in Klammern in der richtigen Reihenfolge in die Lücke und vervollständigen Sie so die **Fragesätze**.

a) ______________________ (I, am) dreaming?

b) ______________________ (you, would, like) to come to my party?

c) ______________________ (they, are) catching the train this evening?

d) ______________________ (we, could, go) to Mary's wedding?

e) ______________________ (we, shall, visit) your cousins?

f) ______________________ (she, can, call) me back?

g) ______________________ (he, does, come) from France?

h) ______________________ (it, is) raining?

203 ★

Geben Sie **Kurzantworten** auf die Fragen aus Übung 202. Verwenden Sie für die Antworten jeweils die Pronomen aus den Fragen.

a) No, ______________.

b) Yes, ______________.

c) No, ______________.

d) Yes, ______________.

e) Yes, ______________.

f) No, ______________.

g) Yes, ______________.

h) No, ______________.

!

Werden **have** und **do** als Vollverben verwendet, werden sie in Fragen und Verneinungen mit **do** umschrieben:

Do you **have** a shower each day? **Does** she **do** her homework carefully?

Wird aber **be** als Vollverb verwendet, dann wird es nicht mit **do** umschrieben:

Is this the band from Glasgow? **Are** you happy?

204 ★

Wählen Sie das jeweils zum Satz passende **Fragewort** aus der Box.

how • why • when • what • who • where • which • whose • how many • what • who

a) ________ saw the accident?

b) ________ happened before the crash?

c) ________ did you like the new café?

d) ________ have you been all day?

e) ________ kids cycle to school?

f) ________ shop in this town sells bikes?

g) ________ did you see? Jenny?

h) ________ has she done today?

i) ________ do you get home?

j) ________ didn't you visit me?

k) ________ bike is green? Yours?

Ist das Fragewort gleichzeitig das Subjekt des Satzes oder ein Teil davon, tritt keine Inversion ein, d. h. es gilt die normale Satzstellung des Aussagesatzes: Fragewort/ Subjekt – Verb – Objekt.

Who wrote *Macbeth*? **Whose cat** bit my dog? **Which of these books** is yours?

205 ★★

Übersetzen Sie die vollständigen Fragen a), b), e), f), g), h) und k) aus Übung 204. Unterstreichen Sie dann jeweils das Subjekt des Satzes.

a) ________________________________

b) ________________________________

e) ________________________________

f) ________________________________

g) ________________________________

h) ________________________________

k) ________________________________

206 ★★

Ordnen Sie den folgenden Sätzen jeweils das passende **question tag** zu.

a) We're going to India, ___ **A** wasn't it?

b) You haven't forgotten your ticket, ___ **B** will you?

c) The pilot is French, ___ **C** didn't she?

d) The hotel was by the sea, ___ **D** does she?

e) Charlie rarely goes jogging, ___ **E** isn't he?

f) You won't need a coat, ___ **F** aren't I?

g) Jane went to the airport, ___ **G** have you?

h) She doesn't eat fish, ___ **H** does he?

i) I'm here, ___ **I** aren't we?

207 ★★

Bilden Sie aus den Vorgaben a), c), d) und g) aus Übung 206 **verneinte Fragen**. Beginnen Sie mit dem Verb des jeweiligen **question tag**.

a) *Aren't we going to India?*

c) ____________________

d) ____________________

g) ____________________

ABC

Die Intonation von **question tags** (= *Bestätigungsfragen*) gibt Auskunft darüber, ob eine echte Antwort erwartet wird oder nicht. Bei fallender Satzmelodie ↓ ist sich der Sprecher seiner Aussage sicher und erwartet keine Antwort. Bei steigender Satzmelodie ↑ (entsprechend der einer echten Frage) erwartet man jedoch eine echte Antwort.

You can swim, **can't you?** ↓ / **can't you?** ↑ *Du kannst schwimmen, nicht wahr?*

208 ★★

Können Sie die folgenden Bitten, Aufforderungen und Vorschläge richtig zusammensetzen? Achtung: Manche enthalten **question tags**!

a) we | out | let's | a business plan | , | shall | work | ?

____

b) you | will | try | this time | to | be | , | punctual | ?

____

c) travelling | Hawaii | how | about | to | next summer | ?

____

d) that | don't | fire extinguisher | , | will | touch | you | ?

____

e) please | won't | come | our wedding | , | to | you | ?

____

209 ★★★

Formulieren Sie die folgenden direkten Fragesätze in **indirekte Fragen** um und beginnen Sie Ihren Satz wie angegeben.

a) How do I get to the railway station?

→ I need to ask ______________________________.

b) Who is visiting us tomorrow?

→ I'd like to know ______________________________.

c) Who have you visited this week?

→ Tell me ______________________________.

210 ★★★

Ergänzen Sie die folgenden **Fragesätze** in der jeweils angegebenen Zeitform und achten Sie dabei besonders auf die Satzstellung.

a) What ______________________________

(haben Sie gemacht; **past progressive***)* before the two cars crashed?

b) When ______________________________

(kam der Krankenwagen an; **past simple***)*?

c) Who ______________________________

(ist zu schnell gefahren; **past progressive***)*?

d) How ______________________________

(ist der Unfall passiert; **past simple***)*?

e) Who ______________________________

(haben Sie gesehen; **present perfect simple***)* today?

211 ★★★

Sie hören im Zug unfreiwillig das Telefongespräch Ihres Sitznachbarn mit. Wie lauten wohl die **Fragen**, die sein Gesprächspartner ihm stellt?

a) ______________________________

I wrote at least 50 letters of application.

b) ______________________________

Yes, I've had some job interviews, and I've even got some job offers.

c) ______________________________

I'm going to accept the job offer from ComputerGames Ltd.

d) ______________________________

I'll start working next week.

212 ★

In der Wortschlange sind acht **Relativpronomen** versteckt. Können Sie sie alle finden?

whateverrlithathuswhoseverwhichowwhowherewhomerwhicheverailewhoeverm

____

____

213 ★

Welcher der beiden angebotenen **Relativsätze** ist jeweils korrekt? Kreuzen Sie an.

a) Our children ...

☐ **A** who were sleeping were quiet.

☐ **B** which were sleeping were quiet.

b) The teacher ...

☐ **A** taught us French was ill.

☐ **B** who taught us French was ill.

c) Tia booked the band ...

☐ **A** that played at our wedding.

☐ **B** who played at our wedding.

d) I got an e-mail ...

☐ **A** whose content was coded.

☐ **B** which content was coded.

214 ★

Wählen Sie aus der Box das richtige **Relativpronomen** aus und setzen Sie es ein. Ein Pronomen kommt zweimal vor.

who • which • whose

a) I don't like dogs ______________ growl at me.

b) That's the boy ______________ ball crashed through our window!

c) Look, there's the shop ______________ I wanted to show you.

d) I know the person ______________ you are talking about.

215 ★

Relativpronomen können Subjekt oder Objekt des **Relativsatzes** sein. Fragen Sie „wer/was“ oder „wen/wem/was“ und übersetzen Sie die Sätze.

a) I've seen the new film with the actor who also played James Bond.

____

b) He's met the girl again who he gave his number to last week.

____

c) Marc had to repair the roof which the storm had damaged.

____

ABC

Whom klingt förmlich und wird meist in der Schriftsprache benutzt.

I was introduced to Mr Long who/**whom** I told that I admired him.

... dem/welchem ...

216 ★★

Wählen Sie das jeweils richtige **Relativpronomen** aus. Manchmal gibt es zwei Möglichkeiten. Entscheiden Sie dann welche der Sätze a)–e) **notwendige Relativsätze** enthalten und welche davon **nicht notwendige Relativsätze**.

a) Brian, **who's / whose** a painter, doesn't earn much.

b) Our neighbours, **who / which** are friendly, help us with the gardening.

c) Who is the man **that / who** got the job?

d) My aunt, **who's / whose** daughter lives in Spain, is flying to Madrid.

e) Colin, **that / who** is a lawyer, has to work long hours.

notwendige Relativsätze: ______________________________

nicht notwendige Relativsätze: ______________________________

217 ★★

Können Sie die **Relativsätze** den passenden Hauptsätzen zuordnen?

a) Look, there's the beautiful garden ___ A who I met seemed to be nice.

b) They visited Jackie's cousin ___ B which were very direct.

c) I was confused by the questions ___ C which I told you about.

d) The man ___ D who lives in New Zealand.

218 ★★

In welchen der **Relativsätze** aus Übung 217 kann das Relativpronomen durch **that** ersetzt werden? In welchen kann es wegfallen?

Ersatz durch **that**: ______________________

Wegfall: ______________________

In notwendigen Relativsätzen kann das Relativpronomen wegfallen, wenn es direktes Objekt oder Präpositionalobjekt des Relativsatzes ist, z. B.:
Is that the bag (**that**/**which**) you bought in Paris last year?

Achtung: In nicht notwendigen Relativsätzen kann das Relativpronomen nicht wegfallen, und der Relativsatz darf nicht mit **that** beginnen.

219 ★★★

Bilden Sie aus den zwei Hauptsätzen je einen **Hauptsatz mit Relativsatz**. Relativpronomen, die wegfallen könnten, setzen Sie in Klammern.

a) Marcus lost his sunglasses. He had only had them for two days.

____

b) Nora has got two new kittens. They are tiny black and white things.

____

c) Joseph ordered a laptop. When it arrived it was broken.

____

220 ★★★

Können Sie die folgenden Sätze ins Deutsche übersetzen?

a) This is the wall on which everybody can pin photos.

---

b) Ms Jones is the woman to whom I sent a letter.

---

c) Here's the museum, behind which you'll find the taxi rank.

---

d) The woman who he was dancing with was French.

---

e) That's the hairdresser in whose salon there's a green carpet.

---

221 ★★★

Die Sätze sind durcheinandergeraten. Achtung: Es handelt sich um **verschiedene Arten von Relativsätzen.**

a) can | he | invite | Lucas | whoever | likes | .

---

b) saved | I | a taxi | which | me | the station | , | a lot of | to | took | stress | .

---

c) his grandma | the house | visited | where | her youth | he | had spent | .

---

d) she | was | stolen | has been using | , | for | her smartphone | which | three months | , | .

---

222 ★

Von den Vorgaben ist jeweils eine richtig. Achtung: Es sind alles ***if*- bzw. *when*-Sätze** mit allgemeingültigen Aussagen.

a) If it rains, you **need / needed** an umbrella.

b) **When** it snows, **when** the streets are dangerous.

c) Water **froze / freezes** if it is colder than 0°C.

d) Please let us know if there **are / were** any problems.

e) When the autumn **will come / comes**, the trees shed their leaves.

f) **If** you cross the street, **if** you need to be careful.

223 ★

Können Sie die ***if*-Nebensätze** den passenden Hauptsätzen zuordnen?

a) If Kay is sick,	___	**A** we can start.
b) If you don't ask Mara,	___	**B** she should stay in bed.
c) If everybody is here,	___	**C** tell him to call me.
d) If you see Gary tonight,	___	**D** she will be disappointed.

224 ★

Die ***if*-Sätze** sind durcheinandergeraten. Können Sie sie wieder ordnen? Achtung: Steht der *if*-Nebensatz vorne, wird er mit einem Komma abgetrennt.

a) If | will | you | complain | don't | sweep | the courtyard | , | Mr Butcher | .

____

____

b) You | have | heard | anything | can | if | tell | you | me | from John | .

____

____

225 ★★

Ordnen Sie die passenden Satzteile einander zu.

a) If you didn't yell at people, ___ **A** they would have listened to you.

b) If you don't yell at people, ___ **B** they would listen to you.

c) If you hadn't yelled at people, ___ **C** they will listen to you.

226 ★★

Wie lauten die korrekten Verbformen in diesen **erfüllbaren *if*-Sätzen**?

a) If we ___ (earn) more money next year, we ___ (travel, can) to Africa.

b) If Mary and Mike ___ (arrive) before 6 p.m., we ___ (go, will) to the cinema.

c) If the film ___ (be) boring, we ___ (watch, can) a DVD instead.

d) If they ___ (want) to eat something, we ___ (order, will) a pizza.

227 ★★

Die folgenden Sätze enthalten **unerfüllbare *if*-Sätze**. Ergänzen Sie auch hier jeweils die richtige Verbform.

a) If I ___ *(hätte)* a million pounds, I ___ *(würde kaufen)* a big house in Mallorca.

b) If we ___ *(flögen)* to Los Angeles, we ___ *(könnten besuchen)* your sister.

c) If you ___ *(kämest)* today, we ___ *(könnten schwimmen gehen)*.

d) If John ___ *(wüsste)* our address, he ___ *(würde uns abholen)*.

e) If she ___ *(nicht spielen würde)* tennis so well, I ___ *(würde spielen)* more often with her.

228 ★★

Bilden Sie aus den Sätzen a)-e) in Übung 227 nun **nicht mehr erfüllbare *if*-Sätze**.

a) *If I had had a million pounds, I would have bought a big house in Mallorca.*

b) ______

c) ______

d) ______

e) ______

229 ★★★

Machen Sie aus folgenden Aussagen ***if*-Sätze**. Achten Sie darauf, ob die Aussage erfüllbar, unerfüllbar oder nicht mehr erfüllbar ist.

a) I can't make it today. There's no train scheduled this evening.

______

b) The dog has bitten you because you scared him.

______

c) This is a nice hotel. I hope it isn't expensive.

______

d) Mike only stopped smoking because his doctor told him to.

______

e) Let's go to the opera. Perhaps tonight's performance is not sold out yet.

______

f) You should invite Kelly. Otherwise Clay will be very disappointed.

______

230 ★★

Welche der ***if*-Sätze** sind Bedingungssätze und welche drücken nur einen Wunsch, eine Bitte oder eine Aufforderung aus? Unterstreichen Sie die Bedingungssätze.

a) If I can get a ticket, I will fly to Italy next week.

b) If you would only stop driving so fast I would feel much better.

c) If you would just call me back as soon as you can ... Thank you.

d) I can book a holiday in the Caribbean if I have time next year.

e) Unless the sun shines, we'll stay indoors.

f) James can visit the Statue of Liberty when he goes to New York.

231 ★★★

Übersetzen Sie die Sätze ins Englische. Achten Sie auf die Wahl der richtigen Zeitformen.

a) *Wenn ich du wäre, würde ich Mandy mit der Reise überraschen.*

____

b) *Wenn Sie mir bitte den Kaffee reichen würden, wäre das sehr nett.*

____

c) *Wenn ich doch nur mehr gereist wäre, als ich noch Zeit dafür hatte.*

____

!

In englischen ***if*-Sätzen** steht niemals **will** oder **would**, außer in höflichen Bitten oder Aufforderungen!

Bedingung mit **if**: **If** his Dad **comes** to his soccer game, Mike **will be** very **happy**.
Bitte mit **if**: **If** you **would** just **like** to sit down over there ...

232 ★

In der Box stehen passive Verbformen, die durcheinander geraten sind. Sie passen zu den untenstehenden Aktivformen. Können Sie sie richtig zuordnen?

evah eben deam • liwl eb tknae • nac eb deus • saw nstloe • sha nebe rwttein • si enbokr

a) stole was stolen
b) break is broken
c) can use can be used
d) have made have been made
e) will take will be taken
f) has written has been written

233 ★

Ordnen Sie die Aktivaussagen den entsprechenden Passivaussagen zu.

a) Jim cut the lawn. ___ A The lawn had been cut by Jim.
b) Jim was cutting the lawn. ___ B The lawn is being cut by Jim.
c) Jim had cut the lawn. ___ C The lawn is cut by Jim.
d) Jim is cutting the lawn. ___ D The lawn was being cut by Jim.
e) Jim cuts the lawn. ___ E The lawn was cut by Jim.

234 ★★

Setzen Sie die Verben in der angegebenen Zeitform im **Passiv** ein. Denken Sie daran, die Hilfsverben jeweils an das Subjekt anzupassen.

a) We ______ (take; **past simple**) to the top level by the lift.

b) The first radios ______ (build; **past simple**) from vacuum tubes.

c) Spiders ______ (fear; **present simple**) by many people.

d) Due to the riots the embassy ______ (close; **present perfect**) since 20th March.

235 ★★

Anweisungen können im Aktiv oder im Passiv formuliert werden. Weisen Sie im **Passiv** an, ...

a) *Gepäck bitte nicht unbeaufsichtigt zu lassen.*

____

b) *eine Nachricht nach dem Ton zu hinterlassen.*

____

236 ★★

Formulieren sie nun die Anweisungen aus Übung 235 im **Aktiv** und überlegen Sie, welche Variante besser klingt.

a) ______________________________

b) ______________________________

237 ★★

Wie lauten die folgenden Aussagen im **Aktiv**?

a) The travellers were led to the cathedral.

____

b) The plane is being boarded now.

____

c) Mia was being laughed at by the class.

____

d) I should have been told by you earlier.

____

Im Passiv sind **progressive forms** nur im **present** und **past tense** gebräuchlich.

The baby **is being carried** around. I **was being driven** home.

238

★★

Wählen Sie die passenden Verbformen aus der Box aus.

can't have been ▪ couldn't have been ▪ might not have been ▪ shouldn't have been ▪ wouldn't have been

I wish the beautiful tree ______________ **(a)** cut down. Although I fear that ______________ **(b)** avoided. Anyway, the new bypass road ______________ **(c)** built in our backyard. The plans ______________ **(d)** put into action if we had protested. But it ______________ **(e)** intended to connect our garage entrance directly to the motorway.

239

★★★

Die folgenden Sätze haben zwei Objekte. Überlegen Sie, aus welchen Sie zwei korrekte, englische **Passivsätze** machen können und, aus welchen einen.

a) The teacher gave me a hint. ______________

____

b) The postman delivered a parcel to our neighbours. ______________

____

c) We offer free drinks to frequent travellers. ______________

____

240

★★★

Ergänzen Sie jeweils den zweiten Satz logisch im **Passiv**.

a) Someone broke into a shop. I wonder what shop ______________.

b) I noticed someone staring at me. I don't like ______________.

c) People say that Caroline is rather shy. – Yes, she ______________.

d) The clerk asked me to fill in the form. All pages had to ______________.

241 ★

Setzen Sie das richtige **Pronomen** in der **indirekten Rede** ein.

a) He thinks: "My time is up." – He thinks that ________ time is up.

b) I tell you: "Your shoelace is untied." – I tell you ________ shoelace is untied.

c) They shout: "We are the people!" – They shout that ________ are the people.

d) We assume: "She is sleeping." – We assume that ________ is sleeping.

!

Pronomen, Zeit- und Ortsangaben müssen an den Standpunkt des Sprechers in der indirekten Rede angepasst werden.

Tim: I will meet **Josie tonight**.
Lisa: Tim said (that) **he** would meet **her that night**.
Josie: Tim said (that) **he** would meet **me that night**.

242 ★

Sind die folgenden Sätze in **indirekter Rede** richtig **(r)** oder falsch **(f)**?

	r	f
a) Tina says she doesn't drink red wine.	☐	☐
b) Everybody knows that wet dogs smelled.	☐	☐
c) Lucas said he asks Dad to explain maths to him.	☐	☐
d) Tim has told me that he is reading *Moby Dick*.	☐	☐
e) They asked me when I had heard of their idea.	☐	☐
f) I had told them I can't come because I have to work.	☐	☐

243 ★★

Wie lauten die Sätze a) und c) aus Übung 241, wenn das einleitende Verb im **past simple** steht?

a) He ____.

c) They ____.

244 ★★

Setzen Sie das in Klammern angegebene Verb in die richtige Zeitform.

a) Columbus didn't believe that the world ________ (be) a disc.

b) When he finally came, I told him that I ________________ (wait) for ages.

c) The teacher told us that Rome ________________ (not build) in a day.

245 ★★

Wie lautet die richtige **Orts- und Zeitangabe in der indirekten Rede**?

a month before • on the phone • that place • the day before • the following year • then • there • those

a) Yesterday, I met Sally in the pub and she asked: "Weren't you already here yesterday?" – She asked whether I had already been

________________________________.

b) "I thought I had told you that on the phone a month ago." – She thought that she had told me that ________________________________.

c) "We'll meet again at this place next year." – We agreed that we would meet again at ________________________________.

d) "I'd like to have some of these cookies now." – I asked if I could have some of ________________ cookies ________________.

246 ★★★

Achtung Glatteis: Tritt bei der Übertragung in die **indirekte Rede** eine Zeitverschiebung (ZV) ein oder nicht? Kreuzen Sie an.

a) "I can't come. My Mom has had an accident." – Barry has told me ... ☐ **ZV**

b) "We were all sorry to hear that." – He had phoned to tell me ... ☐ **ZV**

c) "I would like to travel to India some day." – She told me ... ☐ **ZV**

d) "I hadn't expected to win the lottery." – She said ... ☐ **ZV**

247 ★★

Ordnen Sie die richtigen **indirekten Fragen** bzw. **Aufforderungen** zu.

a) "What did Goethe say?" – He asks me ___ **A** why I quote Goethe.

b) "Did Goethe say that?" – He asks me ___ **B** not to quote Goethe.

c) "How come you quote Goethe?" – He asks me ___ **C** to quote Goethe.

d) "Stop quoting Goethe!" – He asks me ___ **D** whether I quote Goethe.

248 ★★

Schreiben Sie diese direkten Fragesätze in **indirekte** Fragen um.

a) "How do I get to the railway station?"

An elderly man asked us ______________________________.

b) "Where have you put my clothes?"

I asked my husband ______________________________.

c) "Who is visiting us tomorrow?"

My daughter asked me ______________________________.

d) "Who have you visited this week?"

Maya asked her uncle ______________________________.

249 ★★★

Berichten Sie aus Sicht des Babysitters den Eltern am selben Abend von folgendem Dialog. Verwenden Sie dabei ausschließlich die **indirekte Rede**.

Anna: I can't go to bed!

Babysitter: Please, behave and put on your pyjamas.

Anna: My parents told me, "You don't have to put on your pyjamas and you don't have to sleep tonight."

Babysitter: All children need to sleep. Last week you weren't so reluctant.

Anna: That's because last week I had had a nap before you came. But today I'm far too tired to go to bed.

Anna said (that) she couldn't go to bed.

Keine Zeitverschiebung,

1. wenn Ort bzw. Zeit für Sprecher und Berichterstatter (immer noch) gleich sind;
2. bei Gewohnheiten, Naturgesetzen und Tatsachen.

1. "I **like** the area."	I **told** the park ranger that I really **like** the area.
2. Tutor: "A year **has got** 365 days."	The tutor **said** that a year **has got** 365 days.

250 ★★★

Übersetzen Sie die deutschen, direkten Aufforderungen in englische, **indirekte Aufforderungen**.

a) *„Schicken Sie uns das Formular zurück. Ihre Versicherungsgesellschaft."*

b) *Ich sagte zu mir selbst: „Sei stark!"*

c) *Mutter sagte: „Bob, keine Steine werfen!"*

d) *Sie verlangten von mir: „Sei immer vorsichtig!"*

Lösungen

1. SUBSTANTIVE

Geschlecht, Berufe und Anrede

1.
a) w; **b)** m; **c)** w/m; **d)** m; **e)** s; **f)** w/m; **g)** w/m; **h)** s; **i)** w/m; **j)** s; **k)** m; **l)** w/m

2.
a) pilot; **b)** stewardess; **c)** waitress; **d)** shop assistant; **e)** firewoman; **f)** actress; **g)** businesswoman; **h)** authoress; **i)** chemist; **j)** housewife; **k)** dentist; **l)** postwoman

3.
a) The boy is sixteen years old. **b)** The teacher talks to the boy. **c)** The mother calls the boy.

4.
a) countries; **b)** winter holidays; **c)** example; **d)** Germans; **e)** Austria; **f)** Christmas; **g)** New Year's Day; **h)** people; **i)** Netherlands; **j)** journey; **k)** skiing; **l)** French; **m)** Italians; **n)** home; **o)** spring; **p)** run; **q)** hotels; **r)** Alps; **s)** Easter; **t)** Austrian mountains; **u)** same; **v)** Saturdays and Sundays; **w)** February, March and April; **x)** area; **y)** summer months; **z)** travellers; **ab)** city; **ac)** trips; **ad)** Vienna; **ae)** Lake Constance; **ae)** cruises **af)** Danube

5.
a) Professor Schmidt; **b)** Drs Moose; **c)** Mr and Mrs Vogel; **d)** the President of the United States of America

Singular und Plural

6.
a) dresses; **b)** cities; **c)** dishes; **d)** sisters-in-law; **e)** grandchildren; **f)** firewomen; **g)** quizzes; **h)** tomatoes; **i)** fish; **j)** churches

7.
a) two sisters-in-law; **b)** few teeth; **c)** two feet; **d)** a few mice and geese

8.
a) have; **b)** are; **c)** is; **d)** work; **e)** have

9.
a) The police are looking for you!
b) Buy one (pair of) jeans and get one free!
c) These scissors simply cut everything!
d) The news? - ... are on Channel FastFox!

10.
a) B, C; **b)** A, D

11.
a) a slice of, a loaf of; **b)** a piece of, a slice of; **c)** a piece of; **d)** a packet of, a pot of, a cup of; **e)** a bar of, a piece of; **f)** a glass of, a bottle of; **g)** a piece of; **h)** a jar of; **i)** a piece of

12.
a) a lot of/much/any; **b)** enough/much; **c)** some/a lot of/little/no/enough; **d)** some/enough; **e)** a lot of/some/little/enough; **f)** no; **g)** no/little/some/enough/a lot of/not much

13.
a) a lot of; **b)** many; **c)** enough; **d)** much

Genitiv

14.
a) A; **b)** A, B; **c)** B, C; **d)** C

15.
a) H; **b)** F; **c)** A; **d)** C; **e)** B; **f)** G; **g)** D; **h)** E

16.
a) chef's dish; **b)** Jess'(s), kid's rooms; **c)** Jones'(s) tennis rackets; **d)** doctor's, yours; **e)** pilots', wages, airline bosses

17.
a) a friend of my brother's; **b)** Professor Marcus'(s) seminar topics; **c)** some of the most difficult ones; **d)** one of your Professor's courses; **e)** an exam of his/one of his exams; **f)** good friends of his; **g)** a friend of one of Mike's friends; **h)** this (seminar) paper of yours

2. BESTIMMTER UND UNBESTIMMTER ARTIKEL

18.

w	a	s	e	l	f	i	n	d	a
i	d	e	r	m	e	i	n	a	n
e	u	c	e	w	r	d	e	s	v
s	o	d	i	e	s	e	s	w	o
d	e	i	n	r	i	s	u	i	n
e	u	e	e	w	e	s	n	e	v
m	l	f	n	d	e	n	s	e	o

19.

the [ðə] : bank, building, hospital, house, minute, surgery, university
the [ði:] / [ði] : abbey, entrance, hour, institution, object, office, underground

20.

a) a; **b)** an; **c)** a; **d)** an; **e)** a; **f)** a; **g)** an; **h)** a; **i)** an; **j)** an; **k)** an; **l)** an

21.

a) an; **b)** a; **c)** a; **d)** a; **e)** -; **f)** -; **g)** -

22.

a) A; **b)** B; **c)** A; **d)** B; **e)** B; **f)** A; **g)** B; **h)** B

23.

a) F; **b)** E; **c)** G; **d)** A; **e)** C; **f)** H; **g)** B; **h)** D

24.

a) Let's sit in the garden for half an hour.
b) What a nice afternoon with all the flowers in full bloom. **c)** It's quite a surprise that the summer is so warm. **d)** It was such a cold winter last year that the lake froze.
e) Half the number of wasps is flying around compared to last summer.

25.

a) We often drink wine at dinner. I like wine from South Africa. **b)** Life can be exciting. I'm reading a book on the life of Winston Churchill. **c)** Tom will be going to college in the autumn. He'll travel there by bus.
d) I must have forgotten/left my smart-phone on the train. **e)** The food in the hotel was good but I prefer Italian food. **f)** Mia likes to read books. Her husband just reads the paper. **g)** We usually go out for dinner at the weekend.

3. MENGENWÖRTER

26.

a) C; **b)** B; **c)** C; **d)** C

27.

a) any; **b)** some; **c)** some; **d)** some; **e)** any; **f)** some; **g)** any

28.

a) J; **b)** G; **c)** E; **d)** H; **e)** B; **f)** I; **g)** C; **h)** D; **i)** A; **j)** F

29.

a) Grandma hasn't seen a man anywhere outside. **b)** Surely Jane doesn't know anything else about the case. **c)** The police won't ask any questions in the neighbourhood. **d)** The neighbours might not have seen anybody/anyone. **e)** But the man won't already be anywhere else.

30.

a) any; **b)** anywhere; **c)** none; **d)** somewhere; **e)** nobody; **f)** anything; **g)** somebody; **h)** some; **i)** something; **j)** anybody; **k)** nowhere; **l)** nothing

31.

a) Both gardens belong to two most passionate hobby gardeners. **b)** Their gardens are beautiful but the two gardeners are grumblers. **c)** Both of them are retired and now they focus on their hobby. **d)** Neither of them cares to smile at anybody, not even children. **e)** We haven't seen either of them being friendly for years.

32.

a) All; **b)** all the; **c)** all the; **d)** all; **e)** All; **f)** all; **g)** All

33.

a) We bought each of the children an ice-cream. **b)** Each/Every child in the kindergarten loved the visit to the fairy(tale) park. **c)** Everybody/Everyone likes Amy, the friendly kindergarten/nursery school teacher. **d)** Mike goes surfing every weekend in the summer. **e)** Each of the hotel rooms has a separate bathroom. **f)** You can come and see us any time you are in town. **g)** You can take any of the trains or buses to Stuttgart. **h)** At the main station you can ask anybody/anyone to show you the way to the underground.

34.

a) any; **b)** much; **c)** nothing; **d)** few; **e)** somewhere; **f)** neither
Lösungswort: each

4. PRONOMEN UND BEGLEITER

Personalpronomen

35.

F a) We; **E b)** He; **D c)** I; **B d)** you; **C e)** She; **A f)** They

36.

a) me; **b)** it; **c)** her; **d)** us; **e)** it; **f)** her; **g)** it; **h)** her

37.

a) The bank has sent me my bank statement. **b)** The financial adviser gives her customers good advice. **c)** Can you tell me your account number? **d)** The bank cashier was showing me the cash machine. **e)** I gave the bill to my wife. **f)** Ben claims he is faster than me but I am as fast as him.

38.

a) One must be sure of one's facts before one publishes them. **b)** You will never know. **c)** One is not allowed to smoke here/in this lounge. **d)** They/People should meet and find a solution.

Possessivpronomen und -begleiter

39.

his, its, mine, ours, yours, theirs, hers, our, my

40.

a) A; **b)** A; **c)** B; **d)** B; **e)** B; **f)** A

41.

a) Recently Tom didn't have a car of his own. Now he has got one (of his own). **b)** Whose notes are these? Yours or your fellow student's?

Reflexivpronomen

42.

a) himself, (er) sich selbst; **b)** itself, (sie) sich selbst; **c)** themselves, (sie) sich selbst; **d)** himself, (er) sich selbst; **e)** themselves, (sie) sich selbst; **f)** herself, (sie) sich selbst; **g)** themselves, (sie) sich selbst; **h)** yourself, (du/Sie) dich/sich selbst; **i)** ourselves, (wir) uns selbst; **j)** yourselves, (ihr) euch selbst; **k)** itself, (sie) sich selbst

43.

a) F; **b)** G; **c)** L; **d)** I; **e)** H; **f)** B; **g)** K; **h)** J; **i)** D; **j)** A; **k)** C; **l)** E

44.

We planned to build **(a)** a tree house for ourselves **(b)**. When Dad heard about it, he was looking forward to **(c)** helping us. He was surprised **(d)** that we looked at each other **(e)** and had to grin. We imagined **(f)** how Dad would help us with his two left hands. Of course we were pleased **(g)** about his offer. Dad and us, we love each other **(h)**! But it is simply better if Dad keeps away **(i)** from any tools.

Demonstrativpronomen und -begleiter

45.

a) those; **b)** This; **c)** these; **d)** That; **e)** this; **f)** This, that; **g)** these

46.

a) This cheese, **b)** That one; **c)** those (cheeses); **d)** this (bottle/one); **e)** that (bottle/one); **f)** these/those olives; **g)** this/that sushi; **h)** these fish; **i)** those steaks

47.

a) My parents have decided to try this/that new sport. **b)** I planted these yellow flowers myself. Those over there I didn't. **c)** Which one of these blouses shall I buy? This one or that one? **d)** That's our living room over there. Make yourself at home.

5. PRÄPOSITIONEN

48.

a) under(neath); **b)** in; **c)** along; **d)** into; **e)** over/across; **f)** on; **g)** below/in; **h)** across; **i)** through/in; **j)** across/on; **k)** at; **l)** down(wards)

49.

a) on; **b)** above; **c)** under; **d)** on; **e)** between; **f)** in front of; **g)** by; **h)** into; **i)** out of; **j)** to; **k)** round

50.

o	t	n	i	b	e	h	i	n	d
n	o	n	t	o	l	h	o	f	f
e	d	i	s	e	b	t	u	o	r
o	o	e	t	i	s	o	p	p	o
u	n	t	i	l	u	w	o	a	m
t	s	n	i	a	g	a	s	s	o
s	f	a	f	t	e	r	a	t	r
i	o	r	o	u	n	d	n	b	y
d	r	g	i	s	o	s	t	e	t
e	c	n	i	s	g	n	o	m	a

51.

a) B; **b)** B; **c)** C; **d)** A

52.

a) Until; **b)** with; **c)** in; **d)** at; **e)** for; **f)** with; **g)** since; **h)** (a)round; **i)** at; **j)** Before; **k)** in; **l)** between

53.

a) Let's meet in front of the zoo by the pavilion at 9 a.m. on Saturday. **b)** I'd like to go through the greenhouses by 10.30 before it's too hot. **c)** We can walk past the sea lions' pool and go on round the hill. **d)** We can look at the elephants before going into the new ape house. **e)** It has been open for a few weeks since its completion in April. **f)** The opening hours have been from 9 a.m. to 6 p.m. since June.

54.

a) for; **b)** away; **c)** down to; **d)** on; **e)** (-); **f)** up; **g)** into; **h)** apart; **i)** in

55.

a) (r); **b)** (f) chance of; **c)** (f) succeeds in; **d)** (f) worry about; **e)** (r); **f)** (f) difficulty in; **g)** (r); **h)** (f) good at; **i)** (r); **j)** (f) idea of; **k)** (f) interested in; **l)** (r)

6. ZAHLEN

Grund- und Ordnungszahlen

56.

a) four; **b)** nine; **c)** thirteen; **d)** twenty-eight; **e)** eighteen; **f)** fourteen; **g)** twelve; **h)** forty; **i)** fifty-five; **j)** ninety; **k)** nineteen; **l)** one hundred and three; **m)** sixty-nine; **n)** two hundred and seventy-seven;
Lösungswort: twenty-nine

57.

a) 333.3; **b)** 1,760.041; **c)** 12,675.729; **d)** 216,815; **e)** 6,543,211

58.

a) three times three; **b)** once or twice; **c)** hundreds of people; **d)** half an apple; **e)** a hundred times; **f)** two halves; **g)** two and a half kilometres; **h)** three quarters of an hour; **i)** point two five litres; **j)** the twelfth hour; **k)** the German team members came in first, second, eighth and ninth

59.
a) A; **b)** B; **c)** A; **d)** A; **e)** B; **f)** B

Datum und Uhrzeiten

60.
a) It's (a) quarter past six. It's six fifteen (a.m.). **b)** It's twenty to eight. It's seven forty (a.m.). **c)** It's (a) quarter to ten. It's nine forty-five (a.m.). **d)** It's (exactly) one o'clock./It's one p.m. It's thirteen (*AE:* thirteen hundred) hours. **e)** It's twenty-five to four. It's three thirty-five (p.m.)./It's fifteen thirty-five. **f)** It's (a) quarter past four. It's four fifteen (p.m.)./ It's sixteen fifteen. **g)** It's ten past seven. It's seven ten (p.m.)./It's nineteen ten. **h)** It's half past eight. It's eight thirty (p.m.)./It's twenty thirty.

61.
a) in 2001; **b)** on 15th March 44 BC; **c)** in the early and the late 70s; **d)** AD 33; **e)** from 1939 until 1945; **f)** The roaring twenties; **g)** in the year 1929; **h)** in the sixth century

62.
a) July fourth, two thousand (and) twelve; **b)** thirteen minutes to four/three forty-seven (p.m.)/fifteen forty-seven; **c)** the twenty-third of April, nineteen (hundred and) ninety-nine; **d)** seven minutes past eight/eight oh seven (a.m.); **e)** twenty-first November, two thousand (and) thirteen; **f)** the second of May, nineteen (hundred and) fifty-four

7. ADJEKTIVE UND ADVERBIEN

Adjektive

63.
a) an American, the Americans; **b)** a Briton, the British; **c)** a German, the Germans; **d)** a Welshman/-woman, the Welsh; **e)** a Scotsman/-woman, the Scottish; **f)** an Englishman/-woman, the English; **g)** a Portuguese, the Portuguese; **h)** a Spaniard, the Spanish; **i)** a Greek, the Greeks; **j)** a New Zealander, the New Zealanders/the people of New Zealand; **k)** a Dutchman/-woman, the Dutch

64.
a) C; **b)** C; **c)** B; **d)** B

65.
a) Your brother is crazy. Your crazy brother stole my guinea pig! **b)** The heat has turned the milk sour. We can't drink sour milk. **c)** He always tells me to stay calm. I am a calm person. **d)** The bride looks wonderful. She is a wonderful bride.

66.
a) Those ones over there, ... this is a new one on cats. **b)** That sparkling one ..., the three red ones ... **c)** Which ones? These ones right here or those Matisse ones ... this modern one?

67.
a) B; **b)** A; **c)** B; **d)** B

68.
a) The emotional thing ... wonderful ... overwhelming. **b)** The young/Young people ... the elderly/the elderly people ... **c)** The disabled ... everyday/daily life. **d)** The good thing ... the bad thing ... **e)** ... the melodramatic. **f)** ... a disabled person ...

Adverbien

69.
Adverbien: always, extremely, famously, fantastically, often, quietly, simply, still, today

70.
shy - shyly; good - well; hard - hard; late - late; enough - enough; full - fully; new - newly; sure - surely; terrible - terribly; happy - happily; fantastic - fantastically

71.
a) Do you always wash your hair in the shower? **b)** I usually like getting up in the morning. **c)** He never gets home before

7 p.m. **d)** I can seldom find my keys.
e) I don't/do not always have a bath.
f) I don't normally walk to work. **g)** She is sometimes bored with her job.

72.
a) Adjektiv, in a friendly way/manner; **b)** Adjektiv, in a lively way/manner; **c)** Adverb, kind; **d)** Adjektiv, in a deadly manner; **e)** Adjektiv und Adverb, early; **f)** Adjektiv, in a silly way/manner; **g)** Adjektiv, in a lonely way/manner; **h)** Adjektiv und Adverb, daily; **i)** Adverb, rude; **j)** Adjektiv, in a cowardly way/manner; **k)** Adjektiv, in a lovely way/manner

73.
a) very well; **b)** badly paid; **c)** well, Very well; **d)** too late; **e)** nicely styled; **f)** fairly independent; **g)** usually quite friendly; **h)** deeply offended; **i)** horribly; **j)** very rudely lately; **k)** almost certainly never; **l)** quite well

74.
a) My mum/She drives badly. **b)** Antonia/She rides very well. **c)** Mr Clemens/He teaches brilliantly. **d)** Tom/He instructs yoga competently. **e)** My cousin/She/He paints passionately. **f)** Wolfgang/He sails avidly. **g)** Angie/She gardens ingeniously. **h)** José/He plays the guitar fantastically. **i)** Anne/She writes imaginatively.

75.
a) Fortunately Marcie visited us last weekend. **b)** She usually enjoys her visits here. **c)** This time she never really spoke with us./She never really spoke with us this time. **d)** Finally we found out what was troubling her all the time. **e)** Apparently she had lost Grandma's watch somewhere outside/outside somewhere. **f)** It turned out she had simply left it in her gym locker the weekend before. **g)** Now she is going to look after the watch very carefully./She is going to look after the watch very carefully now. **h)** Unfortunately we lost our keys twice last month.

Steigerungsformen und Vergleiche

76.
a) hotter, hottest; **b)** far, further; **c)** simple, simplest; **d)** more, most; **e)** happy, happier; **f)** strong, strongest; **g)** nicer, nicest; **h)** little, least

77.
a) earlier - earliest; **b)** more stupidly - most stupidly; **c)** more often - most often; **d)** more happily - most happily; **e)** harder - hardest; **f)** more slowly - most slowly

78.
a) higher than; **b)** thinner than; **c)** as good as; **d)** more famous than; **e)** busier than; **f)** not as interesting as; **g)** more demanding than

79.
a) biggest; **b)** laziest; **c)** nearest; **d)** most interesting; **e)** worst; **f)** smallest; **g)** best; **h)** most; **i)** narrowest; **j)** most dangerous

80.
a) A; **b)** C; **c)** B; **d)** C

81.
a) The sooner the two of them get married, the better! **b)** On hearing the news she turned as white as a sheet. **c)** My elder sister is a head taller and three years older than me./My elder sister is three years older and a head taller than me. **d)** Run faster than the fastest antelope!

82.
a) Marie plays the violin better than Lisa, but Lisa is the nicest in the group. **b)** Can you pass me that bowl, please? - Which one? The smaller one or the larger one? **c)** Calvin doesn't know less about dinosaurs than Susie although usually she's the cleverest. **d)** Tom cannot/can't swim as fast/quickly as Jerry. But he can jump much/a lot farther/further than Jerry.

83.

a) frequent; **b)** speedy; **c)** early; **d)** clear; **e)** little; **f)** automatic; **g)** far; **h)** friendly; **i)** recent; **j)** clever; **k)** whole; **l)** true

8. VERBEN

Verbformen und Imperativ

84.

a) whisper, whispering; **b)** shout/scream, shouting/screaming; **c)** type, typing; **d)** swim, swimming; **e)** fly, flying; **f)** drive, driving; **g)** lie, lying; **h)** sit, sitting; **i)** run, running

85.

a) shown, past participle; **b)** drank, past simple; **c)** looking, present participle; **d)** chosen, past participle; **e)** run, past participle; **f)** writing, present participle; **g)** ate, past simple

86.

a) sleeping; **b)** closed; **c)** barking; **d)** printed; **e)** shocking; **f)** damaged; **g)** flying; **h)** forgotten

87.

a) Shut the door, please. **b)** Don't forget to tell Josie/Mum to call Mum/Josie. **c)** Never start the mixer when it's open. **d)** Please do not walk on the lawn. **e)** Let's not go to that party. **f)** Let's go to Spain for our holiday this year. **g)** Don't drink/drive and drive/drink. **h)** Take a seat and make yourself comfortable./Make yourself comfortable and take a seat. **i)** Do be back in time for lunch.

88.

a) worked; **b)** cut; **c)** stolen; **d)** play; **e)** throw; **f)** closed; **g)** travelling; **h)** thought; **i)** sew; **j)** to be; **k)** snoozing; **l)** prowling, to call; **m)** Travelling; **n)** went, were; **o)** joking, sailing, taking, tearing

89.

a) A, B; **b)** B; **c)** A, B; **d)** B; **e)** A; **f)** A, B

90.

a) The book ordered last week hasn't come yet. **b)** Bosses openly complaining about their employees aren't popular. **c)** – (Tipp: Das Relativpronomen ist Objekt und nicht Subjekt des Relativsatzes.) **d)** – (Tipp: siehe Hinweis zu c)) **e)** People not smiling when you meet them are disagreeable. **f)** The house sold in our street has been torn down. **g)** Most cats living in the house want to sleep in their owners' beds.

91.

a) Having planned to go on a hiking tour there, we went to Wales last year. **b)** Driving into the mountains, we were surprised by bad weather. **c)** Blinded by the snow, we missed the turning to our B&B. **d)** Found by a local, we still had problems to get to our B&B although he knew the way./Finally we were found by a local knowing the way, but we still had problems to get to our B&B. **e)** Us drinking a grog, our dog was taking a hot bath.

Be, have und *do* und Modalverben

92.

a) have; **b)** are; **c)** am; **d)** has; **e)** are; **f)** is; **g)** does; **h)** do

93.

a) I'm; **b)** they're; **c)** we've; **d)** she's; **e)** he doesn't; **f)** they didn't; **g)** she wasn't; **h)** they weren't; **i)** you aren't/you're not; **j)** she hasn't/she's not; **k)** he's; **l)** you don't

94.

a) does not, D and F; **b)** are not, H; **c)** am, G; **d)** will not, B, C and E; **e)** has been, D and F; **f)** have, A; **g)** would be, B, C and E; **h)** did not, B, C and E

95.

a) shall; **b)** can; **c)** must; **d)** need; **e)** may; **f)** will; **g)** shan't; **h)** can't; **i)** needn't; **j)** needn't; **k)** mustn't , may not; **l)** won't

96.
a) needn't; **b)** mustn't; **c)** may not; **d)** must; **e)** shall; **f)** may; **g)** can't

97.
a) past simple; **b)** present simple; **c)** present perfect; **d)** past simple; **e)** present perfect; **f)** present simple; **g)** present simple

98.
a) No, he won't. **b)** No, they haven't./No, they've not. **c)** No, he didn't. **d)** No, she may not./No, she isn't allowed to. **e)** No, he/she couldn't. **f)** No, I won't. **g)** No, she hasn't. **h)** No, she wasn't. **i)** No, it doesn't. **j)** No, you needn't./No, you don't have to. **k)** No, you needn't. **l)** No, they didn't. **m)** No, you're not./No, you aren't.

99.
would be allowed to; hasn't been supposed to; will have to; should

100.
a) A, C; **b)** B; **c)** A, B; **d)** B

101.
a) E present perfect simple; **b) D** future simple; **c) F** conditional simple; **d) B** present simple; **e) A** past simple; **f) G** present perfect simple; **g) C** past perfect simple

102.
a) want to; **b)** can; **c)** would rather/would prefer to; **d)** couldn't you; **e)** would like to; **f)** Do we have to/Must we/Need we; **g)** was going to; **h)** will you be able to; **i)** ought to; **j)** was to; **k)** might have been; **l)** will we be allowed to, will have been done

103.
a) Did he really have to go? **b)** He could not stay any longer. **c)** He had waited as long as he could. **d)** Is he in a hurry or has he got time? **e)** I would not dare to go near that dog. **f)** You need not worry about him. **g)** How dare you take my car without asking! **h)** We need to go shopping at the weekend. **i)** Were you not doing your homework when I was cooking? **j)** Have you had time to read the report or do you need longer?

104.
a) present perfect simple: can; **b)** past simple: will; **c)** future perfect simple: must; **d)** conditional simple: should; **e)** present perfect simple: may; **f)** conditional perfect simple: can; **g)** future simple: needn't; **h)** past perfect simple: mustn't

105.
<u>Vollverb:</u> **a)**, **b)**, **f)**; <u>Hilfsverb:</u> **c)**, **d)**, **e)**

106.
a) was/were able to do; **b)** has/have been allowed to have; **c)** had been; **d)** will have to be; **e)** would have had; **f)** has/have not been allowed to have; **g)** needs/need to do; **h)** will have done; **i)** would dare to be; **j)** had not had to do

107.
a) I would like to know where Pete is. **b)** He must have missed the plane. **c)** He might/could still be waiting at the airport. **d)** He shouldn't have left so late. **e)** Why can't he ever be on time?/Why can he never be on time?

Gerundien und Infinitive

108.
a) going skiing; **b)** reading; **c)** jogging; **d)** running; **e)** having; **f)** being; **g)** doing

109.
a) no; **b)** yes; **c)** no; **d)** no; **e)** yes; **f)** yes; **g)** yes

110.
a) arriving; **b)** forgetting; **c)** continuing; **d)** opening; <u>Lösung:</u> arguing

111.
a) Cooking new recipes can be risky. (S); **b)** Some friends of my brother's like wrestling./Some of my brother's friends like wrestling. (O); **c)** Training is very important for a good sportsman or -woman. (S); **d)** Max likes to eat a lot. (O); **e)** To write

dozens of postcards on holiday is rather stressful. (S); **f)** Choosing a bride's gown with your mother can be tiring. (S)

112.
a) A, B; **b)** B, C; **c)** B, C; **d)** A, C

113.
gerund: **b), c), f), h), i), m), o), q), r)**
infinitive: **a), d), e), g), j), k), l), n), p)**

114.
a) to miss; **b)** to lose; **c)** to go; **d)** failing; **e)** emptying, to empty; **f)** driving, to drive; **g)** sleeping

115.
a) I was offered several dresses to try on. **b)** A horror movie isn't something to watch before you go to bed. **c)** There's a special code to enter if you want to open the door./ There's a special code which you must enter to open the door. **d)** Sam told me the job to have suited her had been given to Jess. **e)** The best time to handle a problem is not always the earliest.

116.
a) Grandma heard me; **b)** The witness saw the thief; **c)** Mom advised me; **d)** Dad warned me; **e)** I asked my neighbour; **f)** My neighbour noticed two men; **g)** He told them; **h)** All neighbours watched my house

117.
a) She didn't promise to talk about this matter. **b)** She promised not to talk about this matter. **c)** She didn't promise not to talk about this matter. **d)** They are prepared not to talk about the issue. **e)** They are not/ aren't prepared to talk about the issue.

118.
a) The lawn should have been watered. **b)** It also needs to be mowed. (Achtung: Nach *„need"* steht der *passive infinitive*, ins Deutsche wird er jedoch als Aktiv übersetzt.) **c)** Our neighbour seems to be redesigning his garden at last. **d)** Yes, the fence can be repaired.

119.
a) It's no good asking ...; **b)** It's worth trying ...; **c)** It's important to keep ...; **d)** It's not very useful to start ...; **e)** It's unusual for him to come ...; **f)** It's no use complaining ...; **g)** There's no knowing ...; **h)** It's not good to keep ...; **i)** It's a pity for that nice house not to be ...

120.
a) *Ich hörte auf, Radio zu hören, als das Telefon klingelte.* **b)** *Ich hielt an, um meine Mutter vom Friseur abzuholen.* **c)** *Sie erinnerte sich daran, dass sie Briefmarken kaufen musste, als sie an der Post vorbeikam.* **d)** *Sie erinnerte sich, dass sie die Brieftasche bei der Post herausgeholt hatte.* **e)** *Habe ich vergessen, meine Brieftasche zurück in meine Handtasche zu stecken?* **f)** *Ich habe vergessen, dass ich meine Brieftasche ins Handschuhfach anstatt in meine Tasche gelegt hatte.* **g)** *Die Kaninchen versuchten auszubrechen, aber sie versuchten nicht, einen Tunnel zu graben.*

121.
a) me telling; **b)** you to arrive; **c)** me closing; **d)** me to pick; **e)** Chris to watch; **f)** Carol getting

9. ZEITEN

Present simple und progressive

122.
a) works; **b)** goes; **c)** buys; **d)** ask; **e)** explains; **f)** can; **g)** do; **h)** read; **i)** watch; **j)** writes; **k)** does; **l)** helps; **m)** clean; **n)** teach; **o)** says; **p)** like; **q)** has; **r)** tries; **s)** is

123.
a) doing; **b)** running; **c)** smiling; **d)** lying; **e)** travelling (*AE:* traveling); **f)** sitting; **g)** arguing; **h)** swimming; **i)** working; **j)** leaving; **k)** being; **l)** having

124.
a) isn't; **b)** don't; **c)** haven't; **d)** can't; **e)** doesn't; **f)** aren't; **g)** don't work;

h) doesn't stand; **i)** needn't; **j)** am not; **k)** doesn't go; **l)** hasn't

125.
a) is buying; **b)** are standing; **c)** are looking; **d)** is selling; **e)** are checking; **f)** am carrying; **g)** are thinking; **h)** are stumbling; **i)** is running

126.
present simple: always, every day, never, normally, often, sometimes, usually
present progressive: at the moment, just, now, right now, these days, this summer, this week

127.
a) G; **b)** E; **c)** B; **d)** H; **e)** F; **f)** D; **g)** A; **h)** C

128.
a) is taking; **b)** don't have; **c)** goes; **d)** am not

129.
a) takes, isn't going; **b)** go; **c)** are having; **d)** is, causes; **e)** Do ... know, speak; **f)** describes, meet, decide, travel, have; **g)** Isn't ... playing; **h)** is mowing, is helping, is holding, is ... doing, don't cut; **i)** run, am coming

130.
keine progressive form: be, believe, belong, feel, have, hear, know, like, look, see, seem, sound, think, want

131.
a) We are having a party tonight. Right now Mel is working in the kitchen while I am preparing the drinks and cocktails. But I don't know what Jack is doing at the moment. Isn't he taking care of the fire?
b) Terry, I know you don't like spiders, but you are being childish if you don't take this small/little one out yourself.
c) The Johnsons often spend their holidays in Australia. They go diving or sailing and after that they always relax on the beach for a further/another week.
d) You need snow chains in winter in the Alps.

132.
a) Mr Baxter takes the dog out every evening. **b)** Do you always cycle to work in summer? **c)** I do not normally cycle to work when it is cold and wet. **d)** They are often in the garden in the morning./In the morning they are often in the garden.

Past simple und progressive

133.
saw (see), took (take), read (read), went (go), did (do), said (say), made (make), had (have), knew (know), ate (eat), wrote (write), were (be), built (build), drove (drive)

134.
a) spoke; **b)** thought, stayed; **c)** was; **d)** said, worked; **e)** Did, come; **f)** called, changed; **g)** Did, write; **h)** did

135.
a) were, went; **b)** didn't watch; **c)** Did ... have; **d)** went; **e)** put; **f)** gave; **g)** met; **h)** wasn't, had; **i)** didn't make; **j)** Did ... cook; **k)** brought

136.
a) were waiting; **b)** was shining; **c)** was feeling; **d)** was reading; **e)** was playing; **f)** was writing; **g)** were swimming; **h)** Were ... talking

137.
a) What was Mr Marks doing when you noticed a strange noise? – He was telling us off. **b)** What were you doing when a skunk suddenly appeared? – We were trying to escape from Mr Marks. **c)** What was everybody doing when Carol turned up? – Everybody got into a panic about the skunk. **d)** What were you doing when the skunk found you? – I was climbing a tree. **e)** What were Carol and you/you both doing when the power went off? – Carol and I/We were having a shower to get rid of the smell.

138.

a) When did you all notice a strange noise? **b)** When did Mr Marks begin to scream? **c)** When did Carol turn up? **d)** When did the skunk find you? **e)** When did the power go off?

139.

a) Did you have a nice holiday? **b)** Did you play the guitar at the concert? **c)** When I was a child I didn't like reading. **d)** Did they send us an invitation? **e)** We didn't find an invitation in the mail. **f)** Luckily it didn't rain on Lara's birthday. **g)** What did we get as a present for her? **h)** Why didn't Carol go for a walk with the dog?

140.

a) convinced; **b)** quit; **c)** laid; **d)** perceived; **e)** elaborated; **f)** juxtaposed; **g)** negotiated; **h)** stroke; **i)** forbade; **j)** overslept; **k)** resold; **l)** replied

141.

a) was eating; **b)** was hiding; **c)** sneaked; **d)** noticed; **e)** went; **f)** took; **g)** ran

142.

E a) repaired; **F**, **G b)** was looking, sent; **A**, **I**, **C c)** walked, got/caught, was walking/going; **D**, **H**, **B d)** played, drank, lay

143.

a) Did your presentation go down well? – Yes, it did. **b)** What did you do afterwards? – I went to have a drink. **c)** Where did you go to? – I went into that new bar downtown. **d)** How did you like it? – I thought it was brilliant/great.

144.

a) Carol's Mom wasn't happy about them marrying so soon. **b)** When were they sure that they wanted to buy this house? **c)** Josh got acquainted with the estate agent when they both were still at university. **d)** While Josh was laying the carpets, Carol was doing the painting./While Carol was laying the carpets, Josh doing the painting. **e)** The removal van arrived while they were putting the finishing touches to the kitchen. **f)** When the removal men left, Carol and Josh were drinking a glass of champagne./When Carol and Josh were drinking a glass of champagne, the removal men left.

Present perfect simple und progressive

145.

a) had; **b)** made; **c)** answered; **d)** got; **e)** read; **f)** thought; **g)** been; **h)** done; **i)** paid; **j)** watched; **k)** found; **l)** looked

146.

a) she hasn't flown/she's not flown; **b)** he hasn't been flying/he's not been flying; **c)** they haven't worked/they've not worked; **d)** you haven't been managing/you've not been managing; **e)** I haven't done/I've not done; **f)** we haven't started/we've not started (Tipp: Tendenziell wird die Kurzform mit ausgeschriebenem „*not*" eher verwendet, wenn man die Verneinung betonen möchte.)

147.

a) E; **b)** F; **c)** A; **d)** B; **e)** D; **f)** C

148.

a) have felt ill, for; **b)** haven't taken, since; **c)** has had, since; **d)** hasn't eaten, for; **e)** Have you drunk, since; **f)** have enjoyed, since; **g)** have gone, for

149.

a) I've just seen your sister at the hairdresser's. **b)** Haven't they finished doing her hair yet? **c)** She has never looked better in her life. **d)** Have you had a look at the flowers yet? **e)** Have you ever met the bridegroom?

150.

a) have been repairing; **b)** Have you really been waiting; **c)** haven't seen, Have you tried; **d)** Hasn't Jerry been; **e)** have/'ve felt, have/'ve been enjoying; **f)** have/'ve been sitting

Present perfect simple oder past simple?

151.
a) spoken, pp; **b)** began, ps; **c)** seen, pp; **d)** broke, ps; **e)** gone, pp; **f)** drove, ps; **g)** ate, ps; **h)** known, pp; **i)** taken, pp; **j)** forgot, ps

152.
present perfect simple: already, ever, for, just, never, since, so far, this year, until, yet
past simple: ago, in 2001, last year, last week, three years ago, yesterday

153.
a) ran away; **b)** has flown; **c)** swam; **d)** have found, overtook, have taken

154.
a) felt; **b)** have/'ve had; **c)** Have you been ...; **d)** didn't go; **e)** have/'ve cut; **f)** took

155.
a) D; **b)** E; **c)** F; **d)** A; **e)** B; **f)** C

156.
a) When Maya was young she wanted to become a firewoman/firefighter. **b)** Have you ever been in/to Jamaica? **c)** Did you see the thriller when it was on TV? **d)** Sue bought a new house, but she hasn't sold the/her old one yet.

Past perfect simple und progressive

157.
a) being, been; **b)** having, had; **c)** doing, done; **d)** teaching, taught; **e)** learning, learnt; **f)** telling, told; **g)** buying, bought; **h)** keeping, kept; **i)** swimming, swum

158.
a) Yes, they had. **b)** No, she hadn't. **c)** No, he hadn't. **d)** Yes, I/we had. **e)** Yes, you had. (Tipp: bei Selbstgespräch auch: Yes, I had.) **f)** No, we hadn't. **g)** No, they hadn't.

159.
past perfect simple: **b)**, **d)**, **e)**, **f)**
past perfect progressive: **a)**, **c)**, **g)**

160.
a) had been having; **b)** hadn't been reading; **c)** had been raining; **d)** had been late; **e)** had cycled; **f)** hadn't swum

161.
a) had ... been; **b)** been running; **c)** hadn't been arguing; **d)** had been reading; **e)** hadn't thought

162.
a) had been waiting; **b)** had bitten; **c)** had learned/learnt; **d)** had been following

163.
A d) had been studying; **B f)** had read
C b) had been writing; **D c)** fought; **E a)** had roared; **F e)** had been thinking; (Tipp: Bei *„think"* ist normalerweise keine *progressive form* möglich. Hier wird es jedoch wie ein Tätigkeitsverb gebraucht und kann daher im *progressive* stehen.)

Past perfect und past simple

164.
past simple: **b)**, **c)**, **e)**, **g)**
past perfect simple/progressive: **a)**, **d)**, **f)**, **h)**

165.
a) B; **b)** C; **c)** C; **d)** B

166.
a) tread; **b)** spread; **c)** blow; **d)** rise; **e)** forgive; **f)** freeze; **g)** bend
Lösung: delivered

167.
a) had missed, had to wait; **b)** told, had read; **c)** had left, saw, had forgotten; **d)** started, had brought; **e)** arrived, had managed

168.
a) C; **b)** E (B); **c)** D (B); **d)** B; **e)** A

169.
a) has been; **b)** sent; **c)** did ... go; **d)** Have you got; **e)** were talking/talked; **f)** were telling/told; **g)** said; **h)** had looked/had been looking; **i)** found; **j)** Did ... manage

170.
a) Nick has been watching TV since six o'clock. **b)** We had been eating before Andy called to tell us about his baby. **c)** Yesterday evening Tia was having a bubble bath when the doorbell rang.

171.
a) I wasn't working/didn't go to work last week because I got ill on Sunday. **b)** Mia had always lived in Lübeck until she had to move to Oslo last year. **c)** We wanted to visit Thomas but once again he had too much to do.

Future tenses

172.
a) I'm going to have; **b)** she's not going to make; **c)** they're going to do; **d)** Mike's going to travel; **e)** you're not going to stay up; **f)** Mr and Mrs Knox are going to go out

173.
a) Lina won't be here after dinner. **b)** She won't help you with the cooking. **c)** I'm sure the rain will stop soon. **d)** We won't watch a movie tonight. **e)** The Smiths will visit Cádiz.

174.
tomorrow, next year, in ten days, the day after tomorrow, in two years, next month

175.
a) Sam will be going; **b)** they won't be hearing; **c)** she'll have been talking; **d)** I won't have driven; **e)** you'll come back; **f)** it won't sell; **g)** we'll have been doing

176.
a) B; **b)** A; **c)** B; **d)** C

177.
a) If it rains we'll have to take the car. **b)** Is Jim going to help you with your tax return? **c)** The Macks aren't going to spend their holidays in Italy this year./This year the Macks aren't going to spend their holidays in Italy. **d)** Won't Sally be tired after work? **e)** I'll be flying to Cuba tomorrow with Caty./Tomorrow I'll be flying to Cuba with Caty.

178.
a) 'm going to live; **b)** 'll be able to; **c)** 'm taking; **d)** is going to handle; **e)** 'll like; **f)** arrives; **g)** 'll be picking me up

179.
a) is going to be; **b)** will have; **c)** will live; **d)** is coming; **e)** is leaving; **f)** are we going to do

180.
a) C; **b)** F; **c)** A; **d)** E; **e)** B; **f)** D

181.
c) A will have to get up; **f) B** leaves;
e) C are going to have/are having/will have breakfast; **a) D** will have time to relax;
d) E will be taking place/will take place;
b) F will have danced the tango

182.
a) This afternoon I'm seeing the doctor – I have an appointment at 3 p.m. **b)** I don't know exactly where I'm going to spend next summer, but I'd love to/really like to go to France. **c)** If you come round at six I'll have finished gardening by then. **d)** I'm sure you will enjoy your holiday in Turkey next month.

183.
a) will/'ll be visiting; **b)** will/'ll have mown; **c)** will/'ll be having; **d)** will/'ll have saved; **e)** will/'ll have been studying

Conditional und conditional perfect

184.
a) wouldn't she; **b)** should they; **c)** wouldn't he; **d)** wouldn't I; **e)** would you; **f)** would we; **g)** would it

185.
conditional: **a)**, **e)**, **h)**
conditional perfect: **c)**, **f)**, **i)**
past perfect: **b)**, **d)**, **g)**

186.

a) I'd rather ...; **b)** Wouldn't you enjoy ...; **c)** ... wouldn't have been ...; **d)** I'd like ...; **e)** She'd never have come back ...; **f)** What would you do ...

187.

a) would do; **b)** could; **c)** would like; **d)** would be; **e)** could have; **f)** should

188.

a) Would you close the window, please? **b)** In your position I would not tell anybody. **c)** Would she rather go to Rio/London or to London/Rio?

189.

a) wouldn't go; **b)** would not/wouldn't have agreed; **c)** would still be waiting; **d)** would/'d have noticed

10. SATZSTELLUNGEN

190.

a) Dad mows the lawn. **b)** I like her. **c)** Tom can help you./You can help Tom. **d)** I am reading. **e)** The Marksons have invited us. **f)** She is doing her maths homework. **g)** Tilly wants to buy a new car.

191.

a) Jenny, can you help me, please? **b)** ... Yes, I do. **c)** Do you like chips as well? **d)** Please, tell me the truth. **e)** Well, isn't the weather nice today? **f)** ... No, I haven't.

192.

a) A, C; **b)** A, C; **c)** B; **d)** A, B

193.

a) the car; **b)** a single word ... about the whole affair; **c)** the new training course; **d)** everything

194.

a) Jamie, who lives downtown, is meeting us ...; **b)** Dad thought those shoes were too expensive anyway. **c)** Mum was angry yesterday because our dog had slept in Timmy's bed. **d)** Timmy, however, didn't see why he should sleep alone. **e)** Well, it sounds like a good plan but haven't you forgotten a small point? **f)** On the contrary, I think that we have considered everything. **g)** Anyway, I would like to go out for dinner although it's quite late. **h)** Look, there's the restaurant that Marc ...

195.

a) It was the school tennis tournament that Rob won last year. **b)** I can send the CD to you. **c)** It was our neighbours who called the fire brigade when they noticed the smoke.

196.

a) She had hardly opened the door when the cat came in. **b)** Mr Harris introduced the three new maths and physics teachers to us. **c)** Not only did he forget this appointment, but also a lot of others more. (Tipp: Umgangssprachlich wäre auch möglich: He didn't only forget this appointment, but also a lot of others more.) **d)** The car had neither a flat tyre nor any other fault.

197.

a) Lucy fell asleep at kindergarten yesterday afternoon./Yesterday afternoon Lucy fell asleep at kindergarten. (Tipp: Die zweite Variante betont die Zeitangabe.) **b)** Mike usually drives too fast in winter. **c)** The gospel choir sang beautifully at the street party last Saturday.

11. KONJUNKTIONEN

198.

after, where, since, before, and, if, but, because, so, that, when, while, although

199.

a) so that; **b)** because; **c)** When, If; **d)** after; **e)** therefore, so; **f)** while, so

200.
a) I both watch TV and listen to the radio. **b)** I like reading either editorials or the business section. **c)** Today Bill has both read the newspaper and watched a film. **d)** You can have the fish either with boiled potatoes or noodles. **e)** He likes neither swimming nor jogging.

201.
a) As soon as; **b)** Even if/Though; **c)** unless; **d)** Furthermore; **e)** However; **f)** otherwise; **g)** Nevertheless; **h)** though/even if; **i)** as if;

12. FRAGESÄTZE

202.
a) Am I; **b)** Would you like; **c)** Are they; **d)** Could we go; **e)** Shall we visit; **f)** Can she call; **g)** Does he come; **h)** Is it

203.
a) No, I'm not. **b)** Yes, I/we would. **c)** No, they aren't./No, they're not. **d)** Yes, we could. **e)** Yes, we shall. **f)** No, she can't./No, she cannot. **g)** Yes, he does. **h)** No, it isn't.

204.
a) Who; **b)** What; **c)** How; **d)** Where; **e)** How many; **f)** Which; **g)** Who; **h)** What; **i)** When; **j)** Why; **k)** Whose

205.
a) *Wer sah den Unfall?* **b)** *Was passierte vor dem Zusammenstoß?* **e)** *Wie viele Kinder radeln zur Schule?* **f)** *Welcher Laden in dieser Stadt verkauft Fahrräder?* **g)** *Wen hast du gesehen? Jenny?* **h)** *Was hat sie heute gemacht?* **k)** *Wessen Fahrrad ist grün?*

206.
a) I; **b)** G; **c)** E; **d)** A; **e)** H; **f)** B; **g)** C; **h)** D; **i)** F (Achtung: *Question tag* zu „*I am*" lautet „*aren't I*"?)

207.
a) Aren't we going to India? **c)** Isn't the pilot (= he) French? **d)** Wasn't the hotel (= it) by the sea? **g)** Didn't Jane (= she) go to the airport?

208.
a) Let's work out a business plan, shall we? **b)** Try to be punctual this time, will you? **c)** How about travelling to Hawaii next summer? **d)** Don't touch that fire extinguisher, will you? **e)** Please come to our wedding, won't you?

209.
a) I need to ask how I get to the railway station. **b)** I'd like to know who is visiting us tomorrow. **c)** Tell me who you have visited this week.

210.
a) were you doing; **b)** did the ambulance arrive; **c)** was driving too fast; **d)** did the accident happen; **e)** have you seen

211.
a) How many letters of application did you write? **b)** Have you had any job interviews yet (or even some offers)? **c)** Which of the job offers are you going to accept? **d)** When will you start working?

13. RELATIVSÄTZE

212.
whatever, that, whose, which, who, whom, whichever, whoever

213.
a) A; **b)** B; **c)** A; **d)** A

214.
a) which; **b)** whose; **c)** which; **d)** who

215.
a) *Ich habe den neuen Film mit dem Schauspieler gesehen, der/welcher auch James Bond gespielt hat.* **b)** *Er hat das Mädchen wieder getroffen, dem/welchem er letzte Woche seine Nummer gegeben hat.* **c)** *Marc musste das Dach reparieren, das/welches der Sturm letzte Woche beschädigt hatte.*

216.
a) who's; **b)** who; **c)** who/that; **d)** whose; **e)** who
notwendige Relativsätze: **c)**
nicht notwendige Relativsätze: **a)**, **b)**, **d)**, **e)**

217.
a) C; **b)** D; **c)** B; **d)** A

218.
Ersatz durch *that*: **a)**, **b)**, **c)**, **d)**
Wegfall: **a)**, **d)**

219.
a) Marcus lost his sunglasses (which/that) he had only had for two days. **b)** Nora has got two new kittens which/that are tiny black and white things. **c)** Joseph ordered a laptop which/that was broken when it arrived.

220.
a) *Dies ist die Wand, an die jeder Fotos heften kann.* **b)** *Frau Jones ist die Frau, an die ich einen Brief geschickt habe.* **c)** *Hier ist das Museum, hinter welchem Sie den Taxistand finden.* **d)** *Die Frau, mit der/welcher er tanzte, war Französin.* **e)** *Das ist der Friseur, in dessen Salon ein grüner Teppich liegt.*

221.
a) Lucas can invite whoever he likes.
b) I took a taxi to the station, which saved me a lot of stress. **c)** He visited the house where his grandma had spent her youth.
d) Her smartphone, which she has been using for three months, was stolen.

14. *IF*-SÄTZE

222.
a) need; **b)** When it snows, the streets are dangerous. **c)** freezes; **d)** are; **e)** comes; **f)** If you cross the street, you need to be careful.

223.
a) B; **b)** D; **c)** A; **d)** C

224.
a) If you don't sweep the courtyard, Mr Butcher will complain. **b)** You can tell me if you have heard anything from John.

225.
a) B; **b)** C; **c)** A

226.
a) If we earn more money next year, we can travel to Africa. **b)** If Mary and Mike arrive before 6 p.m., we will go to the cinema.
c) If the film is boring, we can watch a DVD instead. **d)** If they want to eat something, we will order a pizza.

227.
a) If I had a million pounds, I would buy a big house in Mallorca. **b)** If we flew to Los Angeles, we could visit your sister. **c)** If you came today, we could go swimming. **d)** If John knew our address, he would pick us up.
e) If she didn't play tennis so well, I would play more often with her.

228.
a) If I had had a million pounds, I would have bought a big house in Mallorca. **b)** If we had flown to Los Angeles, we could have visited your sister. **c)** If you had come today, we could have gone swimming. **d)** If John had known our address, he would have picked us up. **e)** If she hadn't played tennis so well, I would have played more often with her.

229.
a) If there was a train scheduled this evening, I would make it today. **b)** If you hadn't scared the dog, it wouldn't have bitten you. **c)** If it hadn't been expensive, it would have been a nice hotel. **d)** Mike wouldn't have stopped smoking if his doctor hadn't told him to. **e)** We'll go to the opera if tonight's performance isn't sold out.
f) If you don't invite Kelly, Clay will be very disappointed.

230.
Bedingungssätze: **a)**, **d)**, **e)**, **f)**

231.
a) If I were you, I would surprise Mandy with the trip. (Tipp: In der Umgangssprache heißt es auch oft: *If I was you, ...*) **b)** If you would please hand/pass me the coffee, that would be very nice. **c)** If only I had travelled more when I still had the time for it.

15. PASSIV

232.
a) was stolen; **b)** is broken; **c)** can be used; **d)** have been made; **e)** will be taken; **f)** has been written

233.
a) E; **b)** D; **c)** A; **d)** B; **e)** C

234.
a) were taken; **b)** were built; **c)** are feared; **d)** has been closed

235.
a) Luggage must not be left unattended.
b) A message can be left after the tone.

236.
a) Please don't leave your luggage unattended. **b)** Please leave a message after the tone. (Tipp: Anweisungen im Passiv wirken zwar strenger, sind jedoch nicht unbedingt wirkungsvoller und werden eher als unfreundlich empfunden.)

237.
a) They /He/She led the travellers to the cathedral.
b) They are boarding the plane now.
c) The class was/were laughing at Mia.
d) You should have told me earlier.

238.
a) wouldn't have been; **b)** couldn't have been; **c)** shouldn't have been; **d)** might not have been; **e)** can't have been

239.
a) I was given a hint by the teacher./
A hint was given to me by the teacher.
b) A parcel was delivered to our neighbours (by the postman). **c)** Free drinks are offered to frequent travellers (by us)./Frequent travellers are offered free drinks (by us).

240.
a) I wonder what shop was broken into.
b) I don't like being stared at. **c)** Yes, she is said to be shy. **d)** All pages had to be filled in.

16. INDIREKTE REDE

241.
a) his; **b)** your; **c)** they; **d)** she

242.
a) r; **b)** f (... that wet dogs smell.); **c)** f (Lucas said he asked Dad ...); **d)** r (keine Zeitverschiebung nach einleitendem Verb im *present perfect*); **e)** r; **f)** f (... I couldn't come because I had to work. (Zeitverschiebung nach einleitendem Verb im *past perfect*)

243.
a) He thought that his time was up.
c) They shouted that they were the people.

244.
a) was; **b)** had been waiting; **c)** wasn't/was not built

245.
a) there the day before; **b)** on the phone a month before; **c)** that place the following year; **d)** those, then

246.
a) keine Zeitverschiebung wegen einleitendem Verb im *present perfect;*
b) Zeitverschiebung wegen einleitendem Verb im *past perfect;* **c)** keine weitere Zeitverschiebung von Verben im *conditional* möglich; **d)** keine weitere Zeitverschiebung von Verben im *past perfect* möglich

247.

a) C; **b)** D; **c)** A; **d)** B

248.

a) An elderly man asked us how to get to the railway station. **b)** I asked my husband where he had put my clothes. **c)** My daughter asked me who would be visiting us tomorrow/the next day. **d)** Maya asked her uncle who he had visited this week/that week. (Tipp: Zeitangaben werden in der indirekten Rede beibehalten, wenn der betreffende Zeitraum für den Sprecher noch nicht zu Ende ist. Andernfalls verschieben sich die Angaben oder sie werden durch konkrete Daten in der Vergangenheit ersetzt.)

249.

Anna said (that) she couldn't go to bed. I told her to behave and to put on her pyjamas. She said (that) you had told her that she didn't have to put on her pyjamas and (that) she didn't have to sleep tonight. I told her (that) all children need to sleep and (that) she hadn't been so reluctant last week. She said (that) that was because she had had a nap last week before I came but (that) today she was far too tired to go to bed.

250.

a) My/Our insurance company wanted me/us to return the form. **b)** I told myself to be strong. **c)** Mother told/asked Bob not to throw stones. **d)** They wanted me to always be careful.

Wortverzeichnis

Abkürzungen:

Abk.	Abkürzung	**etw.**	etwas	**Pl.**	Plural (Mehrzahl)
AE	amerikanisches Englisch	**jdm.**	jemandem	**sb**	somebody
BE	britisches Englisch	**jdn.**	jemanden	**sth**	something

A

a.m. (*Abk.* für ante meridiem)	*morgens (bei Uhrzeiten)*
abbey	*Abtei(kirche)*
able	*fähig*
about	*über; um; an*
above	*über, oberhalb*
abroad	*im Ausland*
to **abuse**	*missbrauchen*
to **accept**	*annehmen, akzeptieren*
accident	*Unfall*
account	*Konto*
accurate	*genau*
to **achieve**	*erreichen*
acquainted	*bekannt*
across	*über, jenseits, auf der anderen Seite von*
action	*Handlung*
actor, actress	*Schauspieler, Schauspielerin*
AD (*Abk.* für Anno Domini)	*n. Chr., Anno Domini*
addicted	*süchtig*
to **address**	*adressieren; ansprechen*
to **admire**	*bewundern*
advance	*Fortschritt*
to **advance**	*voranschreiten*
adventure	*Abenteuer*
advice	*Rat(schlag)*
to **advise**	*(be)raten*
adviser	*Berater(in), Ratgeber(in)*
affair	*Angelegenheit*
afraid	*verängstigt, Angst haben*
Africa	*Afrika*
after	*nach*
again	*wieder*
against	*gegen*
age	*Alter*
ages	*Ewigkeiten; Zeitalter (Pl.)*
ago	*vor (zeitlich)*
to **agree**	*zustimmen, einverstanden sein*
alike	*gleich; ähnlich*
alley	*Gasse*
to **allow**	*erlauben*
almost	*fast*
alone	*allein*
the **Alps**	*die Alpen*
already	*schon*
also	*auch*
although	*obwohl*
always	*immer*
American	*Amerikaner/in; amerikanisch*
angry	*wütend, verärgert*
another	*noch ein(e, r)*
to **answer**	*(be)antworten*
antelope	*Antilope*
anxious	*besorgt*
any	*(irgend)ein(e); etwas*
anybody	*jede(r); (irgend)jemand*
anymore	*weitere(n); mehr*
anyone	*(irgend)ein(e)*
anything	*(irgend)etwas*
anyway	*sowieso; jedenfalls*
anywhere	*irgendwo*
apart	*auseinander*
ape	*Affe*
to **appear**	*erscheinen*
application	*Bewerbung*
appointment	*Verabredung, Termin*
to **approve**	*billigen, zustimmen*
area	*Gebiet*
to **argue**	*argumentieren; streiten*
an **argument**	*ein Argument; ein Streit*
around	*um ... herum*
to **arrive**	*ankommen*
article	*Artikel*
as	*als, wie*
as well	*auch*
to **ask**	*fragen, bitten*
asleep	*schlafend*
to **assume**	*annehmen, vermuten*
to **attack**	*angreifen*
attic	*Dachboden*
Australia	*Australien*
Austria	*Österreich*
Austrian	*Österreicher(in); österreichisch*
author	*Schriftsteller(in)*
automatically	*automatisch*
avid	*eifrig, begeistert*
to **avoid**	*vermeiden*
away	*entfernt, weg, fort*
awful	*schrecklich*

B

backyard	*Hinterhof (BE); Garten (AE)*
baker	*Bäcker(in)*
bar	*Bar; Stange; Riegel; Streifen*
barbecue	*Grill; Grillparty*
barefoot	*barfuß*
to **bark**	*bellen*
basket	*Korb*
bath	*Bad, Badezimmer*
BC (*Abk.* von before Christ)	*v. Chr.*

beach	*Strand*
bear	*Bär*
beautiful	*schön*
to **become**	*werden*
beef	*Rindfleisch*
beer	*Bier*
before	*vor*
to **begin**	*anfangen*
to **behave**	*(sich) benehmen*
behind	*hinter*
bend	*Kurve*
Belgian	*Belgier(in); belgisch*
to **believe**	*glauben*
to **belong**	*gehören*
to **bend**	*biegen*
better	*besser*
between	*zwischen*
bike	*Fahrrad*
bite	*Bissen, Biss*
bill	*Rechnung*
billion	*Milliarde*
bin (BE)	*Mülltonne, Mülleimer*
bird	*Vogel*
birth	*Geburt; Abstammung, Herkunft*
bit	*Stück, Teil; bisschen*
to **bite**	*beißen*
blade	*Klinge*
blank	*leer, blank; ausdruckslos*
blinded	*geblendet*
bloom	*Blüte*
blouse	*Bluse*
to **board**	*einsteigen, (Flugzeug) besteigen*
to **boil**	*kochen*
bone	*Knochen*
to **book**	*buchen*
bored	*gelangweilt*
boring	*langweilig*
to **borrow**	*sich etw. von jdm. leihen*
both	*beide(s)*
bottle	*Flasche*
bride's gown	*Brautkleid*
bread	*Brot*
to **break**	*(zer)brechen*
to **break out**	*ausbrechen*
break-in	*Einbruch*
breath	*Atemzug; Atem*
to **bring**	*bringen*
Britain	*Britannien*
bubble	*Blase, Seifenblase*
to **bubble**	*sprudeln, kochen, brodeln*
to **build**	*bauen*
building	*Gebäude*
burglar	*Einbrecher(in)*
burgundy	*burgunderrot; Burgunderwein*
to **burn**	*(ver)brennen*
businessman	*Geschäftsmann*
butcher	*Metzger(in)*
by	*von; neben; während*
by hand	*von Hand*
bypass (road)	*Umgehung(sstraße)*

C

cake	*Kuchen*
call	*Anruf*
to **call**	*(an)rufen*
calm	*ruhig*
campsite	*Campingplatz*
Canada	*Kanada*
canary	*Kanarienvogel*
to **cancel**	*stornieren*
to **care**	*sich kümmern, sich sorgen*
careful	*vorsichtig*
caretaker	*Hausmeister(in)*
carnival	*Karneval*
carpet	*Teppich*
carrot	*Möhre*
to **carry**	*tragen*
case	*Fall*
cash	*Bargeld*
cashier	*Kassierer(in)*
catalogue	*Katalog*
to **catch**	*fangen*
cathedral	*Kathedrale*
Catholic	*Katholik(in); katholisch*
cause	*Ursache*
central	*zentral*
centre (BE), **center** (AE)	*Zentrum*
century	*Jahrhundert*
certain	*sicher*
champagne	*Champagner*
to **change**	*ändern, wechseln*
channel	*Kanal*
to **check**	*überprüfen*
cheers	*prost, danke schön, tschüss*
cheese	*Käse*
chef	*Koch, Köchin*
chemist	*Apotheker(in); Chemiker(in)*
cherry	*Kirsche*
chess	*Schach*
to **chide**	*schelten, tadeln*
child, children (Pl.)	*Kind, Kinder*
chips	*Pommes frites*
choir	*Chor*
to **choose**	*wählen*
Christmas	*Weihnachten*
church	*Kirche*
cinema	*Kino*
to **circulate**	*zirkulieren*
city	*(Groß-)Stadt*
claim	*Anspruch*
to **clean**	*reinigen*
clear	*klar*
clerk	*Büroangestellte(r), Rezeptionist(in)*
to **climb**	*klettern*
clock	*Uhr*
to **close**	*schließen*
closely	*eng, nah*
clothes	*Kleidung*
club	*Verein, Klub*
coach	*Trainer(in)*
coat	*Mantel*

Wortverzeichnis

code	*Code, Kennzahl*
coffeeshop	*Café*
cold	*kalt; Kälte*
colleague	*Kollege, Kollegin*
college	*Hochschule*
comfortable	*bequem*
common	*gemeinsam*
compared	*verglichen*
compartment	*Fach; Abteil(ung)*
competent	*kompetent, fähig*
to **complain**	*(sich be)klagen*
completely	*vollständig*
completion	*Abschluss*
to **concentrate**	*(sich) konzentrieren*
concert	*Konzert*
conditional	*bedingt; Konditional*
to **confuse**	*verwirren*
to **connect**	*verbinden*
to **consider**	*betrachten, überlegen*
constantly	*ständig*
construction	*Bau*
content	*Inhalt*
to **continue**	*fortsetzen, etw. weiterhin tun*
contrary	*Gegenteil*
convertible	*umwandelbar; Kabrio(lett)*
to **convince**	*überzeugen*
cookie (AE)	*Plätzchen, Keks*
corner	*Ecke*
to **cough**	*husten*
could	*könnten*
country	*Land*
course	*Kurs*
courtyard	*(Innen-)Hof*
cowardly	*feige*
crash	*Absturz; Unfall; Zusammenstoß*
crazy	*verrückt*
crisis	*Krise*
to **cross**	*überqueren*
crowded	*überfüllt*
cruise	*Kreuzfahrt, Reise*
cupboard	*Schrank*
curious	*neugierig*
curl	*Locke*
customer	*Kunde, Kundin*
to **cut**	*schneiden*
to **cycle**	*radeln*

D

dachshund	*Dackel*
daily	*täglich*
to **damage**	*beschädigen*
to **dance**	*tanzen*
dangerous	*gefährlich*
to **dare**	*wagen*
dark	*dunkel*
data	*Daten*
date	*Datum*
Danube	*Donau*
deadly	*tödlich*
deafening	*ohrenbetäubend*
to **decide**	*entscheiden*
deep	*tief*
definitely	*definitiv*
delivered	*geliefert*
to **demand**	*fordern, verlangen*
dentist	*Zahnarzt, Zahnärztin*
department store	*Kaufhaus*
to **describe**	*beschreiben*
desk	*Schreibtisch*
detailed	*detailliert*
detergent	*Waschmittel*
devil	*Teufel*
to **die**	*sterben*
difference	*Unterschied*
difficulty	*Schwierigkeit*
to **dig (out)**	*(aus)graben*
dirty	*schmutzig*
disagreeable	*unangenehm*
to **disappear**	*verschwinden*
disappointed	*enttäuscht*
disc	*Scheibe (z.B. CD, DVD)*
to **discuss**	*diskutieren*
dish	*Gericht (Essen)*
to **dislike**	*nicht mögen*
to **disturb**	*stören*
DIY (*Abk. für* do-it-yourself)	*heimwerken*
documents	*Unterlagen*
doorbell	*Türklingel*
downtown (AE)	*Innenstadt*
dozen	*Dutzend*
to **dream**	*träumen*
dress	*Kleid*
to **drive**	*fahren*
driver	*Fahrer(in)*
dry	*trocken*
due to	*durch, wegen*
during	*während*
dust	*Staub*
dustbin	*Mülltonne*

E

each	*jede(r, s) (einzelne)*
early	*früh*
to **earn**	*verdienen*
earth	*Erde*
Easter	*Ostern*
editorial	*Leitartikel*
egg	*Ei*
either	*entweder; jede(r, s) (von beiden); auch*
elaborate	*kompliziert, aufwändig; sorgfältig*
elder	*ältere(r, s)*
the **elderly**	*(die) Senioren*
electric	*elektrisch*
electronic	*elektronisch*
elementary	*elementar, Grund-*
else	*sonst*
embassy	*Botschaft*
employee	*Mitarbeiter(in), Beschäftigte(r)*
empty	*leer*
engine	*Motor*
English	*Englisch; englisch; Engländer(in)*
to **enjoy**	*genießen*

enough	*genug*
to **enter**	*eingeben; betreten*
entrance	*Eingang*
equipment	*Ausrüstung*
equivalent	*Äquivalent, Entsprechung*
to **escape**	*flüchten*
estate agent	*Immobilienmakler(in)*
Europe	*Europa*
even	*sogar*
event	*Ereignis*
eventually	*schließlich*
ever	*jemals*
every	*jede(r, s)*
everybody	*alle*
everything	*alles*
exam	*Prüfung*
excellent	*ausgezeichnet*
exchange	*Austausch*
exciting	*spannend*
to **expect**	*erwarten*
expensive	*teuer*
to **explain**	*erklären*
to **explore**	*erkunden*
extinguisher	*Feuerlöscher*
extremely	*äußerst*

F

fact	*Tatsache*
to **fail**	*scheitern*
fair	*Messe; gerecht; blond*
to **fall**	*fallen*
famous	*berühmt*
far	*weit*
fascinating	*faszinierend*
fashionable	*modisch*
fast	*schnell*
fast-forward	*Vorspultaste*
to **fear**	*fürchten*
favour	*Gefallen*
favourite	*Favorit, Lieblings-*
fear	*Angst*
feather	*Feder*
fee	*Gebühr*
to **feel**	*fühlen*
female	*weiblich*
fence	*Zaun*
ferry	*Fähre*
festivity	*Fest*
to **fetch**	*holen*
fever	*Fieber*
few	*wenige, ein paar*
fifties (1950s)	*fünfziger Jahre*
fight	*Streit*
to **fight**	*kämpfen; streiten; bekämpfen*
file	*Datei*
to **fill (in)**	*(aus)füllen*
finally	*schließlich*
financial	*Finanz-*
to **find**	*finden*
farther	*weiter (entfernt)*
fine	*fein*
to **finish**	*beenden*
finishing touch	*der letzte Schliff*
fire	*Feuer*
fire brigade (BE)	*Feuerwehr*
firefighter, fireman, firewoman	*Feuerwehrmann, Feuerwehrfrau*
firm	*Firma*
to **fit**	*passen*
fixed-term	*befristet*
flat	*Wohnung*
flight	*Flug*
flock	*Herde*
flower	*Blume*
fluently	*fließend*
to **fly**	*fliegen*
to **focus on**	*sich konzentrieren auf*
to **follow**	*folgen*
food	*Essen, Nahrung*
food processor	*Küchenmaschine*
football	*Fußball*
for example	*zum Beispiel*
to **forbid**	*verbieten*
to **forget**	*vergessen*
to **forgive**	*vergeben*
fortunately	*zum Glück*
France	*Frankreich*
free	*kostenlos; frei*
to **freeze**	*einfrieren; frieren*
French	*Französisch; französisch; Franzose, Französin*
frequent	*häufig*
fresh	*frisch*
fridge	*Kühlschrank*
friendly	*freundlich*
from	*aus*
fruit	*Obst*
fuel	*Kraftstoff*
full	*voll*
fun	*Spaß*
funky	*flippig, abgefahren*
furniture	*Möbel*
furthermore	*außerdem*
further	*weiter (entfernt), ferner*
future	*Zukunft*

G

game	*Spiel*
to **garden**	*gärtnern*
gardener	*Gärtner(in)*
generous	*großzügig*
German	*Deutsch; deutsch; Deutsche(r)*
gerund	*Gerundium*
to **get**	*erhalten*
to **get rid of sb/sth**	*jdn./etw. loswerden*
to **get up**	*aufstehen*
glove	*Handschuh*
to **go out**	*ausgehen*
goal	*Ziel; Tor*
gospel choir	*Gospelchor*
gossip	*Klatsch*
gown	*Kleid*
grandchild	*Enkel(in)*
grandma	*Oma*
Greece	*Griechenland*
greedily	*gierig*
greenhouse	*Gewächshaus*
to **grin**	*grinsen*

Wortverzeichnis

to **grow**	*wachsen*
to **growl**	*knurren*
grumbler	*Nörgler(in)*
to **guess**	*erraten*
guest	*Gast*
guinea pig	*Meerschweinchen*
guitar	*Gitarre*
guy	*Kerl*
gym	*Turnhalle*

H

hair	*Haar*
hairdresser, hairdresser's	*Friseur(in), Friseursalon*
half	*Hälfte*
hammock	*Hängematte*
handbag	*Handtasche*
to **handle**	*behandeln*
to **hang out**	*aufhängen*
to **happen**	*geschehen, passieren*
hard	*schwer*
hardly	*kaum*
hat	*Hut*
to **hate**	*hassen*
headache	*Kopfschmerzen*
to **hear**	*hören*
heat	*Wärme*
heating	*Heizung*
help	*Hilfe*
to **help**	*helfen*
helpful	*hilfreich; hilfsbereit*
hers	*ihres*
hero	*Held(in)*
herself	*sich (selbst)*
to **hide**	*verstecken*
high	*hoch*
hiking tour	*Wanderausflug, Wanderung*
himself	*sich (selbst)*
hint	*Hinweis*
to **hold**	*halten; besitzen*
home	*Zuhause*
homework	*Hausaufgaben*
honour	*Ehre*
to **hope**	*hoffen*
horrible	*schrecklich*
horse	*Pferd*
hospital	*Krankenhaus*
hot	*heiß*
hour	*Stunde*
househusband, housewife	*Hausmann, Hausfrau*
however	*jedoch*
to **hunt**	*jagen*
to **hurry**	*sich beeilen*
hurt	*verletzt*
husband	*Ehemann*
hut	*Hütte*

I

icy	*eisig*
if	*wenn, falls*
ill	*krank*
imaginative	*fantasievoll, einfallsreich*
important	*wichtig*
impossible	*unmöglich*
impression	*Eindruck*
impressive	*beeindruckend*
incident	*Vorfall*
to **include**	*umfassen*
independent	*unabhängig*
India	*Indien*
indoors	*drinnen*
infinitive	*Infinitiv*
information	*Informationen*
ingenious	*genial*
instead	*stattdessen*
institution	*Institution*
instructor	*Ausbilder(in)*
to **insult**	*beleidigen*
to **intend**	*beabsichtigen*
interested in	*interessiert an*
interesting	*interessant*
interruption	*Unterbrechung*
into	*in (hinein)*
to **introduce**	*vorstellen*
intruder	*Eindringling*
invitation	*Einladung*
to **invite**	*einladen*
irritable	*reizbar*
isle	*(kleine) Insel*
issue	*Thema, Frage; Ausgabe*
Italian	*Italienisch; italiensich; Italiener(in)*
Italy	*Italien*
itself	*sich (selbst)*

J

jam	*Marmelade*
jar	*Glas*
to **jog**	*joggen*
to **join**	*beitreten, mitmachen*
journey	*Reise*
just	*nur*
to **juxtapose**	*nebeneinanderstellen, gegenüberstellen*

K

to **keep**	*(be)halten*
key	*Schlüssel; Taste*
kid (AE)	*Kind, Jugendliche(r)*
kind	*Art*
kindly	*freundlich*
to **kitten**	*Kätzchen*
to **knit**	*stricken*
to **know**	*wissen*
known	*bekannt*

L

lake	*See*
landlady	*Wirtin*
language	*Sprache*
last	*letzte(r, s)*
to **last**	*(an)dauern*

	late	*spät*
	lately	*in letzter Zeit*
to	**laugh**	*lachen*
	lawn	*Rasen*
	lawnmower	*Rasenmäher*
	lawyer	*Anwalt, Anwältin*
to	**lay**	*legen*
	lazy	*faul*
	leaflet	*Broschüre*
to	**learn**	*lernen*
	least	*am wenigsten*
to	**leave**	*verlassen*
	lecture	*Vortrag*
	less	*weniger*
to	**let**	*lassen, zulassen, erlauben*
	let's	*lass(t) uns, lassen Sie uns*
	letter	*Brief*
	level	*Ebene*
	liberty	*Freiheit*
	licence	*Lizenz, Erlaubnis*
	lie	*Lüge*
	lift	*Aufzug*
	light	*Licht*
	light-blue	*hellblau*
	lightning	*Blitz*
	lights	*Beleuchtung*
	like	*wie*
	line	*Linie*
	lion	*Löwe*
to	**listen**	*hören*
	lively	*lebendig*
	loaf	*Laib*
	local	*lokal, örtlich*
to	**located**	*gelegen*
	loch	*See*
	locked	*verschlossen*
	locker	*Schließfach*
	lonely	*einsam*
to	**look**	*aussehen; schauen; suchen*
to	**look forward to sth**	*sich auf etw. freuen*
	lorry	*Lastwagen, LKW*
to	**lose**	*verlieren*
a	**lot (of), lots of**	*viel(e), eine Menge*
	lottery	*Lotterie*
	loudly	*laut*
	lounge	*Lounge, Warteraum*
	lovely	*schön*
	low	*niedrig*
	Ltd (*Abk. von* Limited)	*GmbH*
	luck	*Glück*
	luckily	*glücklicherweise*
	luggage	*Gepäck*

M

	mail	*Post*
	main	*Haupt-*
	male	*männlich*
to	**manage**	*verwalten*
	manner - place - time	*Art und Weise - Ort - Zeit*
	many	*viele*
	map	*(Land-)Karte*
	marketplace	*Marktplatz*
	marriage	*Ehe*
	married	*verheiratet*
to	**marry**	*heiraten*
	matter	*Angelegenheit, Sache*
to	**matter**	*von Bedeutung sein*
	may	*können, dürfen*
	mayor	*Bürgermeister(in)*
	meal	*Mahlzeit*
to	**mean**	*bedeuten*
	media	*Medien*
	medicine	*Medizin*
to	**meet**	*treffen*
	menu	*Speisekarte; Menü*
	message	*Nachricht*
	microwave	*Mikrowelle*
	might	*könnten (vielleicht)*
	mind	*Geist, Verstand*
	mine	*mein(e, r, s)*
	mineral	*Mineral-*
	misconception	*falsche Vorstellung*
	missed	*verpasst*
	mobile (phone) (BE), **cell(ular) (phone)** (AE)	*Mobiltelefon, Handy*
	mole	*Maulwurf*
	moon	*Mond*
	moss	*Moos*
	mossy	*moosig*
	most	*am meisten*
	motorbike	*Motorrad*
	motorway	*Autobahn*
	mountain	*Berg*
	mouth	*Mund*
	mouth-watering	*sehr appetitlich, köstlich*
	move	*Bewegung*
to	**move**	*(sich) bewegen; umziehen*
	movie (AE), **film** (BE)	*Film*
to	**mow**	*mähen*
	mower	*Mäher*
	much	*viel*
	murdered	*ermordet*
	must	*müssen*
	must not/mustn't	*nicht dürfen*
	myself	*mir; mich (selbst)*

N

	nap	*Nickerchen*
	narrow	*eng*
	near	*in der Nähe von*
	necessary	*erforderlich*
	need	*brauchen*
	need not/needn't	*nicht brauchen, nicht müssen*
	negative	*negativ*
to	**negotiate**	*verhandeln*
	neighbour	*Nachbar(in)*
	neighbourhood	*Nachbarschaft*
	neither (... nor)	*weder (... noch)*
	nerve	*Nerv*
the	**Netherlands**	*die Niederlande*
	never	*nie(mals)*
	nevertheless	*dennoch*
	New Year's Day	*Neujahr*

Wortverzeichnis

New Zealand	*Neuseeland*
news	*Nachrichten*
newspaper	*Zeitung*
next	*nächste(r, s)*
nice	*schön, nett*
nobody	*niemand*
noise	*Lärm*
none	*keine(r, s)*
noodle	*Nudel*
noon	*Mittag*
nor	*noch*
normally	*normalerweise*
northern	*Nord-*
not ... anything	*nicht alles*
not ... either	*auch nicht*
note	*Notiz*
to **note**	*bemerken*
nothing	*nichts*
notice	*Bekanntmachung*
noun	*Nomen, Substantiv*
novel	*Roman*
now	*jetzt*
nowhere	*nirgends*
number	*Zahl, Ziffer; Anzahl*

O

o'clock	*... Uhr (in Zeitangaben)*
object	*Objekt*
occupation	*Beruf; Beschäftigung*
occupied	*besetzt*
to **occur**	*auftreten*
off	*aus; weg ... von*
offence	*Vergehen*
offended	*beleidigt*
offer	*Angebot*
to **offer**	*anbieten*
office	*Büro*
often	*oft*
oil	*Öl*
once	*einmal*
the **ones**	*diejenigen*
oneself	*sich (selbst)*
only	*nur*
onto	*auf (... hinauf)*
to **open**	*öffnen*
opening	*Öffnungs-; Eröffnung*
openly	*offen*
opera	*Oper*
opinion	*Meinung*
to **opt**	*sich für etw. entscheiden*
optimist	*Optimist(in)*
to **order**	*bestellen*
organized	*organisiert, geordnet*
other	*andere(r, s)*
otherwise	*sonst, andernfalls*
ours	*unsere(r, s)*
ourselves	*uns selbst*
out of order	*kaputt, außer Betrieb*
outside	*außerhalb*
over	*über*
overcrowded	*überfüllt*
to **over-fertilize**	*überdüngen*
to **oversleep**	*verschlafen*
to **overtake**	*überholen*
own	*eigene(r, s)*
to **own**	*besitzen*
owner	*Eigentümer(in)*

P

p.m. (*Abk. für* post meridiem)	*nachmittags/abends (bei Uhrzeiten)*
packet	*Paket, Päckchen, Packung*
page	*Seite*
paid	*bezahlt*
to **paint**	*malen*
painter	*Maler(in)*
painting	*Malerei; Gemälde*
palace	*Palast*
panic	*Panik*
paper	*Papier*
parcel	*Paket*
parents	*Eltern*
participle	*Partizip*
party	*Partei*
to **pass**	*bestehen (z.B. Prüfung)*
passionate	*leidenschaftlich*
passive	*passiv*
past	*Vergangenheit*
pavilion	*Pavillon*
to **pay**	*zahlen, bezahlen*
PE (*Abk. für* physical education)	*Sport (als Unterrichtsfach)*
people	*Menschen, Leute*
to **perceive**	*wahrnehmen*
perfect	*perfekt; Perfekt*
perhaps	*vielleicht*
phone	*Telefon*
to **phone**	*telefonieren, anrufen*
phrasal verb	*Verb mit Präposition oder Adverb*
physics	*Physik; Physik-*
to **pick**	*wählen*
piece	*Stück*
pig	*Schwein*
to **pin**	*befestigen, anheften*
pity	*Mitleid*
place	*Ort*
placed	*platziert*
to **plan**	*planen*
plane	*Flugzeug*
plenty	*reichlich*
point	*Punkt*
the **police**	*Polizei*
policewoman, policeman	*Polizistin, Polizist*
poor	*arm*
pope	*Papst*
popular	*beliebt*
pork	*Schweinefleisch*
possible	*möglich*
to **post**	*(per Post) schicken*
postcard	*Postkarte*
postman	*Postbote*
pot	*Topf*
potato	*Kartoffel*
pothole	*Schlagloch*
pound	*Pfund*
power	*Macht; Strom, Energie*
power cut	*Stromausfall*
to **practise**	*üben*

to **prefer**	*bevorzugen*
to **prepare**	*vorbereiten*
present	*Gegenwart; Geschenk; derzeitig*
press	*Presse*
pretty	*ziemlich; hübsch*
to **prevent**	*verhindern*
previous	*früher*
price	*(Kauf-)Preis*
to **print**	*drucken*
prize	*Preis (Gewinn)*
probably	*wahrscheinlich*
processed	*verarbeitet*
progressive	*Verlaufs-; fortschreitend*
to **promise**	*versprechen*
to **promote**	*fördern; befördern; für etw. werben*
proposal	*Vorschlag*
Protestant	*Protestant(in); protestantisch, evangelisch*
to **prowl**	*(umher) streifen*
pub	*Kneipe*
to **pull**	*ziehen*
punctual	*pünktlich*
pupil	*Schüler(in)*
to **put**	*setzen, stellen, legen*
pyjamas	*Pyjama, Schlafanzug*

Q

quarter	*Quartal; Viertel(-)*
queue	*(Warte-)Schlange, Reihe*
quick	*schnell*
quiet	*ruhig*
quietness	*Ruhe*
to **quit**	*beenden*
quite	*ziemlich; ganz, völlig*
to **quote**	*zitieren*

R

rabbit	*Kaninchen*
racket	*(Tennis-)Schläger*
raft	*Floß*
rafting tour	*Rafting-/Wildwassertour*
railway	*Eisenbahn*
rain	*Regen*
to **rain**	*regnen*
to **raise**	*erhöhen*
ranger	*Ranger(in), Aufseher(in)*
rank	*Rang*
rapidly	*schnell*
rarely	*selten*
raspberry	*Himbeere*
rat	*Ratte*
rather	*eher, lieber*
to **reach**	*erreichen*
ready	*bereit; fertig*
to **realize**	*erkennen, sich einer Sache bewusst werden*
really	*wirklich*
reception	*Empfang*
recipe	*(Koch-)Rezept*
redesigned	*neu gestaltet*
to **refuse**	*verweigern*
to **regret**	*bedauern*
regularly	*regelmäßig*
relationship	*Beziehung*
relieved	*erleichtert*
reluctant	*widerwillig, widerstrebend*
to **rely on**	*sich auf jdn. verlassen*
to **remain**	*(zurück)bleiben*
to **remember**	*sich merken, sich erinnern an*
removal firm	*Umzugsfirma*
to **rent**	*mieten*
to **repair**	*reparieren*
to **repeat**	*wiederholen*
to **reply**	*antworten*
report	*Bericht*
to **require**	*erfordern*
to **research**	*(er)forschen*
to **resell**	*weiter/wieder verkaufen*
to **resent**	*sich über jdn./etw. ärgern, etw. übelnehmen*
responsible	*verantwortlich*
retired	*im Ruhestand*
retirement	*Ruhestand*
return	*Rückkehr; Erstattung*
ride	*Fahrt*
rider	*Fahrer(in); Reiter(in)*
to **ride**	*reiten; fahren (z.B. Fahrrad, Motorrad)*
right	*Recht*
to **ring**	*klingeln*
riot	*Aufruhr, Unruhen*
risky	*riskant*
rival	*Rivale, Rivalin*
river	*Fluss*
road	*Straße*
to **roar**	*brüllen*
Roman	*Römer(in); römisch*
romantic	*Romantiker(in); romantisch*
Rome	*Rom*
roof	*Dach*
rose	*Rose*
round	*Runde*
row	*Reihe*
rubbish	*Müll*
rude	*unhöflich*
rudely	*grob*
rule	*Regel*
to **run**	*laufen, rennen*
runaway	*Ausreißer(in)*
rush	*Ansturm*

S

safe	*sicher*
to **sail**	*segeln*
sailor	*Seemann, Matrose*
salad	*Salat*
salt	*Salz*
same	*gleich*
sausage	*Würstchen*
to **save**	*sparen; retten*
saw	*Säge*

Wortverzeichnis

scarcely	*kaum*
scared	*verängstigt*
scene	*Szene*
schedule	*Zeitplan*
Scotland	*Schottland*
Scottish	*schottisch*
to **scream**	*schreien*
screen	*Bildschirm*
scuba-diver	*Sporttaucher(in)*
sculpture	*Skulptur*
sea(bed)	*Meer(esboden)*
season	*Saison; Jahreszeit*
seat	*Sitz*
secretary	*Sekretär(in)*
secret	*Geheimnis*
section	*Abschnitt*
to **seem**	*scheinen*
seldom	*selten*
to **sell**	*verkaufen*
to **send**	*senden, schicken*
to **separate**	*trennen*
series	*Serie*
several	*mehrere*
severe	*schwer*
shall	*werden, sollen*
to **share**	*teilen*
sheet	*Blatt (Papier)*
shelf	*Regal*
shift	*Schicht*
to **shine**	*glänzen*
ship	*Schiff*
shipping	*Versand*
shirt	*Hemd*
shocked	*schockiert*
shoelace	*Schnürsenkel*
shop assistant	*Verkäufer(in)*
to **shout**	*rufen*
to **show**	*zeigen*
shower	*Dusche*
to **shut**	*schließen*
shy	*schüchtern*
sick	*krank*
side	*Seite*
sideboard	*Anrichte*
sight	*Blick, Sicht, Sehkraft, Sichtweite*
silly	*albern*
since	*seit*
single	*einzig(e, r); einzeln, Einzel-; allein, Allein-*
sister-in-law	*Schwägerin*
site	*Standort*
sixties (1960s)	*sechziger Jahre*
skiing	*Skifahren, Skilauf*
skirt	*Rock*
skunk	*Stinktier*
slice	*Scheibe*
smell	*Geruch*
to **smell**	*riechen*
smile	*Lächeln*
smoke	*Rauch*
smoking	*Rauchen*
to **sneak**	*schleichen*
to **sniff**	*schnüffeln*
snow	*Schnee*
so	*so, also*
soccer	*Fußball*
soil	*Boden*
soldier	*Soldat(in)*
solution	*Lösung*
to **solve**	*lösen*
somebody, someone	*(irgend)jemand*
something	*etwas*
sometimes	*manchmal*
somewhere	*irgendwo*
soon	*bald*
sooner	*früher*
sorry	*leid tun; traurig, bedauernswert; Entschuldigung*
sort	*Art*
to **sound**	*klingen*
soup	*Suppe*
sour	*sauer*
Spain	*Spanien*
sparkling	*funkelnd; prickelnd*
sparkling wine	*Sekt*
special	*besondere(r, s)*
speedily	*schnell*
to **spend**	*verbringen; verbrauchen*
spider	*Spinne*
sports	*Sport*
sportsman, sportswoman	*Sportler, Sportlerin*
spot	*Stelle*
to **spread**	*verbreiten*
spring	*Frühling*
the **same**	*der/die/das Gleiche; der-/die-/dasselbe*
stable	*Stall*
stall	*(Markt-/Verkaufs-) Stand*
stamp	*Briefmarke*
to **stand**	*stehen*
to **stare**	*starren*
statement	*Erklärung*
station	*Station; Bahnhof*
statistics	*Statistik*
to **stay**	*bleiben*
to **steal**	*stehlen*
steamy	*dunstig, dampfig*
steward, stewardess	*Flugbegleiter, Flugbegleiterin*
still	*immer noch; ruhig, still*
storm	*Sturm*
strange	*seltsam*
strawberry	*Erdbeere*
street	*Straße*
stressful	*stressig*
to **strike**	*schlagen*
to **study**	*studieren, lernen*
to **stumble (over)**	*stolpern (über)*
stupid	*dumm*
styled	*gestylt, herausgeputzt*
to **succeed**	*Erfolg haben, erfolgreich sein*
success	*Erfolg*
such	*so; solche(r, s); derartig*
suddenly	*plötzlich*
to **suggest**	*vorschlagen*
suitable	*geeignet*
to **suit**	*passen*

sunburn	*Sonnenbrand*
sunglasses	*Sonnenbrille*
to **suppose**	*vermuten*
sure(ly)	*sicher(lich)*
surgery	*Arztpraxis, Sprechstunde; Chirurgie, chirurgischer Eingriff*
surprise	*Überraschung*
to **surprise**	*überraschen*
to **sweep**	*fegen*
sweets	*Süßigkeiten*
to **swim**	*schwimmen*
Switzerland	*Schweiz*
Syria	*Syrien*

T

tablet	*Tablette*
tag	*Anhänger, Etikett*
to **take**	*nehmen*
to **take care (of sth/sb)**	*sich (um etw./jdn.) kümmern*
to **take place**	*stattfinden*
tall	*groß, hoch (gewachsen)*
to **taste**	*schmecken, probieren*
tax	*Steuer, Abgabe*
taxi driver	*Taxifahrer(in)*
to **teach**	*lehren, unterrichten*
teacup	*Teetasse*
to **tear down**	*abreißen (Gebäude)*
television (TV)	*Fernsehen*
to **tell**	*erzählen; sagen*
tennis tournament	*Tennisturnier*
tense	*Zeitform*
terrace	*Terrasse*
terrible	*schrecklich*
the **Thames**	*die Themse*
than	*als (in Vergleichen)*
to **thank**	*danken*
that	*dass*
theirs	*ihre(r, s)*
themselves	*sie (Pl.) (sich selbst)*
therefore	*deshalb*
these	*diese (Pl.)*
thief	*Dieb(in)*
those	*jene (Pl.)*
though	*obwohl*
throat infection	*Halsentzündung*
through	*durch*
to **throw**	*werfen*
tides	*Ebbe und Flut, Gezeiten*
tidy	*ordentlich*
tie	*Krawatte*
tiny	*winzig*
tired	*müde*
tiring	*ermüdend*
together	*zusammen*
ton	*Tonne (Gewicht)*
tool	*Werkzeug*
top	*Dach*
top level	*oberstes Stockwerk*
to **touch**	*berühren*
the **Tower (of London)**	*der Tower (von London)*
town	*Stadt*
town hall	*Rathaus*
traffic	*Verkehr*
train	*Zug*
training	*Ausbildung*
to **travel**	*reisen*
travel agent	*Reisebüroangestellte(r)*
traveller	*Reisende(r)*
tricycle	*Dreirad*
trifle	*Trifle (geschichtetes Dessert); Kleinigkeit*
to **tread**	*treten*
troubling	*beunruhigend*
true	*wahr*
truly	*wirklich, wahrhaftig*
truth	*Wahrheit*
to **try**	*versuchen*
trip	*Trip, Reise*
tube	*Rohr; Londoner U-Bahn*
to **turn as white as a sheet**	*weiß wie die Wand werden*
to **turn on**	*anschalten*
to **turn up**	*auftauchen, erscheinen*
turning	*Abbiegung*
twenties (1920s)	*zwanziger Jahre*
twice	*zweimal*
the **Twin Towers**	*Zwillingstürme des ehemaligen World Trade Centers in New York*
twins	*Zwillinge*
type	*Typ*

U

umbrella	*Regenschirm*
uncountable	*unzählbar*
underground	*U-Bahn*
to **understand**	*verstehen*
unexpected	*unerwartet*
unfortunately	*leider*
unfriendly	*unfreundlich*
union	*Gewerkschaft*
university	*Universität*
the **United States (of America)**	*die Vereinigten Staaten (von Amerika)*
unless	*es sei denn*
to **unlock**	*entriegeln, aufschließen*
to **untie**	*lösen, aufbinden*
until	*bis*
unusual	*ungewöhnlich*
unwell	*unwohl*
urn	*Urne*
to **use**	*verwenden*
used to do sth	*früher etw. (gerne) getan haben*
useful	*nützlich*
usually	*in der Regel*

V

vacation (AE), **holiday** (BE)	*Urlaub*
to **vacuum**	*staubsaugen*
vacuum tube	*Elektronenröhre*
van	*Lieferwagen*
vegetable	*Gemüse*
visitor	*Besucher(in)*
Vienna	*Wien*

Wortverzeichnis

W

wage	*Lohn*
waiter, waitress	*Kellner, Kellnerin*
to **wake**	*wecken*
to **walk**	*gehen*
wallet	*Portemonnaie, Geldbeutel*
to **want**	*wollen*
warmly	*herzlich*
to **warn**	*warnen*
the **washing**	*Wäsche*
washing machine	*Waschmaschine*
wasp	*Wespe*
to **watch**	*beobachten, schauen*
to **water**	*gießen, bewässern*
watering	*Bewässerung*
watermelon	*Wassermelone*
wedding	*Hochzeit*
well	*gut; nun (ja)*
wet	*nass*
whether	*ob*
which	*welche(r, s); der, die, das*
while	*während*
whoa	*langsam, hoppla*
whoever	*wer auch immer*
whole	*ganze(r, s)*
wholly	*ganz, völlig*
whose	*deren, dessen; wessen*
wife	*Ehefrau*
will	*werden*
to **win**	*gewinnen*
wine	*Wein*
wire	*Stromkabel; Draht*
to **wish**	*wünschen*
to **withdraw**	*abheben (Geld); sich zurückziehen*
without	*ohne*
witness	*Zeuge, Zeugin*
to **wonder**	*sich fragen*
wonderful	*wunderbar*
worker	*Arbeiter(in)*
world	*Welt*
World War II	*Zweiter Weltkrieg*
to **worry**	*sich sorgen*
worth	*wert*
would	*würden*
wrestling	*Ringen*
writer	*Schriftsteller(in)*

Y

to **yell**	*schreien*
yet	*bis jetzt; schon; noch*
yours	*dein, Ihr, euer*
yourself	*du (dich selbst), Sie (sich selbst), ihr (euch selbst)*
youth	*Jugend(lichkeit); Jugendliche(r)*

2 WORTVERZEICHNIS

Bildnachweis

S. 13: shutterstock/Preto Perola, b) fotolia/Andrey Armyagov, c) fotolia.de/nougaro, d) shutterstock/ffolas, e) fotolia/jeanphilippe delisle, f) shutterstock.com/Lakhesis, g) istockphoto.com/Louis Aguinaldo, h) shutterstock/matka_Wariatka, i) istockphoto.com; S. 18: a) Fotolia.com/Aaron Amat, c) iStockphoto/Peter Petto, e) shutterstock/ID1974, g) Fotolia.com/endostock, i) iStockphoto/Simon Smith, k) shutterstock/intoit; S. 28: A) shutterstock/Marcin Balcerzak, B) shutterstock/bluefox, C) Shutterstock/Minerva Studio, D) fotolia/paffy, E) Fotolia.com/Alexander Raths, F) shutterstock/Goodluz; S. 34: a) Fotolia.com/HLPhoto, b) shutterstock/Africa Studio, c) fotolia.de/April D; S. 35: d) Fotolia.com/luckylight, e) shutterstock/mrfotos, f) istockphoto.com/Vitalina Rybakova, g) shutterstock/Fanfo, h) shutterstock/artproem, i) fotolia/kreativfabrik1; S. 36: a) istockphoto/Resavskyi, b) istockphoto/PK-Photos, c) fotolia/James Peragine, d) fotolia/Elena Moiseeva, e) iStockphoto/DeadDuck, f) fotolia.de/Mikael Damkier, g) fotolia/Bikeworldtravel, h) shutterstock/zhaoliang70, i) fotolia/HaBlu, j) shutterstock/holbox, k) fotolia/Petair, l) shutterstock/Dudarev Mikhail; S. 44: istockphoto.com/Rasmus Rasmussen, a) - h) PONS GmbH, Stuttgart; S. 57: a) istockphoto/Marcel Braendli, b) istockphoto.com/Ischa Gast, c) iStockphoto/Morten Elm, d) istock/Viktor1; S. 60: a) fotolia.de/lunamarina, b) istockphoto.com/Sergey Rusakov, c) istockphoto.com/malerapaso, d) fotolia/HaBlu, e) fotolia/Eray, f) istockphotophoto/himalaja, g) istockphoto.com/Liv Friis-Larsen, h) shutterstock.com/Brasiliao, i) shutterstock/Joyce Marrero; S. 78: fotolia/Rostislav Ageev; S. 95: A) fotolia/Djordje Korovljevic, B) fotolia.de/Dudarev Mikhail, C) thinkstockphotos.com/Getty Images, D) fotolia.de/yanlev, E) fotolia/jörn buchheim, F) thinkstockphotos/BananaStock, G) fotolia.de/Aaron Amat, H) fotolia/beerfan, I) shutterstock/kalim; S. 106: A) iStockphoto/franckreporter, B) iStockphoto/craftvision, C) Fotolia.com/shefkate, D) shutterstock/ID1974, E) fotolia/jamenpercy, F) istockphoto/michele princigalli; S. 115: a) istockphoto.com/Ischa Gast, b) Fotolia.com/Forgiss, c) istockphoto.com, d) fotolia.de/MNStudio, e) fotolia.de/Elenathewise, f) fotolia.de/Andrew Barker